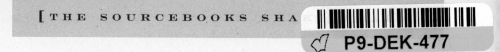

P9-DEK-477

Macbeth

TEXT EDITOR
WILLIAM PROCTOR WILLIAMS

ADVISORY EDITORS
DAVID BEVINGTON, PETER HOLLAND, AND MICHAEL KAHN

SERIES EDITORS
MARIE MACAISA AND DOMINIQUE RACCAH

William Shakspeare

sourcebooks
mediaFusion

An Imprint of Sourcebooks Inc.®
Naperville, Illinois

Audio and photo credits can be found at the end of the book.

Published by Sourcebooks MediaFusion, an imprint of Sourcebooks, Inc.
P.O. Box 4410, Naperville, Illinois 60567-4410
(630) 961-3900
Fax: (630) 961-2168
www.sourcebooks.com
www.sourcebooksshakespeare.com
For more information on The Sourcebooks Shakespeare, email us at
shakespeare@sourcebooks.com.

LIBRARY OF CONGRESS CATALOGING-IN-PUBLICATION DATA

SHAKESPEARE, WILLIAM, 1564-1616.
  MACBETH / WILLIAM SHAKESPEARE ; TEXT EDITOR, WILLIAM PROCTOR WILLIAMS.
    P. CM.
  INCLUDES BIBLIOGRAPHICAL REFERENCES AND INDEX.
  ISBN-13: 978-1-4022-0688-7 (ALK. PAPER)
  ISBN-10: 1-4022-0688-7 (ALK. PAPER)
  1. MACBETH, KING OF SCOTLAND, 11TH CENT.--DRAMA. 2. SCOTLAND--KINGS
AND RULERS--DRAMA. 3. REGICIDES--DRAMA. 4. SHAKESPEARE, WILLIAM,
1564-1616. MACBETH. I. WILLIAMS, WILLIAM PROCTOR, 1939- II. TITLE.

PR2823.A2W59 2006
822.3'3--DC22

2006018317

Printed and bound in the United States of America.
LB 10 9 8 7 6 5 4 3 2 1

To students, teachers, and lovers of Shakespeare

Contents

About Sourcebooks MediaFusion vi

About the Text vii

On the CD xi

Featured Audio Productions xv

Note from the Series Editors xvii

In Production: *Macbeth* Through the Years 1
by William Proctor Williams

As Performed: By the Royal Shakespeare Company 11
at the Swan Theatre in Stratford-upon-Avon in 1999
by Gregory Doran

"Hours Dreadful and Things Strange": 21
Macbeth in Popular Culture
by Douglas Lanier

MACBETH BY WILLIAM SHAKESPEARE 37

The Cast Speaks: The 2004–05 Cast from the 267
Shakespeare Theatre Company
by Marie Macaisa

A Voice Coach's Perspective on Speaking Shakespeare: 283
Keeping Shakespeare Practical
by Andrew Wade

In the Age of Shakespeare 291
by Thomas Garvey

About the Online Teaching Resources 303

Acknowledgments 305

Audio Credits 307

Photo Credits 309

About the Contributors 311

About the Text

Macbeth, probably written in 1606, is the shortest of all of Shakespeare's tragedies and one of the shortest of all his plays. The only early text of the play is that which was printed in the First Folio (F1) edition of his *Comedies, Histories, and Tragedies* in 1623, and that is the basis for the present edition. The manuscript copy for F1 was almost certainly a document of theatrical origins, though probably not the performance script (prompt book or allowed book) used by the King's Men, Shakespeare's acting company. One indication of this is that many of the stage directions found in F1, such as the opening stage direction of Act 1, Scene 7 ("*Hautboys and torches. Enter a Sewer, and divers Servants with dishes and service, and pass over the stage. Then enter Macbeth*"), show the sort of brevity one might expect from a document created for practical use in the theatre. The acts and scenes divisions in F1 have, in most cases, been observed in this edition. Note, however, that these divisions would have been of no importance at public theaters, such as the Globe, where playing was continuous, nor at the private theaters, such as the Blackfriars, where only act divisions would have been observed (in order to trim the candles needed for lighting).

Act 5, always seen by editors as difficult, presents a special case. In F1, this act is divided into seven scenes, but editors since Alexander Pope in 1725 have opted for eight, nine, and even ten scenes by rigidly (and for nontheatrical reasons, I believe) adhering to the rule that when the stage is cleared, a scene is concluded. Thus, in the final battle (5.5–5.7 in this edition) editors started a new scene every time all the combatants exit fighting even though they reenter still in battle. On stage, these fight scenes would have formed one *continuous* set of actions, tied together by trumpet calls and by actors entering as others exit. Therefore, this edition follows the original scene divisions of F1.

The composition (typesetting) and printing of F1, for the most part, is of typical accuracy for the time. Though there is some confusion about characters' names early in the play (when the compositors did not yet know the full names and titles of some persons), the major question with the text has always been the lineation. Since F1 always begins a new verse line at the left margin, whether the line is a full line or part of a line, editors have had to decide which ones are single short lines and which ones are lines to be shared. 1.5.56–58 provides and illustration of the problem. In F1 this reads:

Duncan comes here to Night.
Lady. And when goes hence?
Macb. To morrow, as he purposes.
Lady. O never,
Shall Sunne that Morrow see

In this edition, and in many modern editions, this becomes:

Duncan comes here tonight.
LADY MACBETH
                And when goes hence?   56

MACBETH
Tomorrow, as he purposes.

LADY MACBETH
                O, never   57
Shall sun that morrow see.   58

Here 56 and 57 are shared part lines while 58 is a short line by itself. Over the last three hundred years of editing, various editors have dealt with this matter in a number of ways. In this edition, I have treated part lines as shared when it seems that one characters is answering, responding to, or completing the thought of another character and as single, unshared lines when this does not appear to be the case. These sorts of editorial decisions are what account for the variation in line numbers from modern edition to modern edition. To provide a fixed and unvarying point of reference, Through-Line-Numbering (TLN) is supplied at the foot of every left-hand (notes) page indicating the TLNs to be found in this portion of text. TLN was a system devised by Charlton Hinman for *The Norton Facsimile: The First Folio of Shakespeare* (1968) and this system numbers every line of type in F1, thereby providing a fixed system of reference. Since critics, scholars, and editors increasingly use TLNs in their references, sometimes in conjunction with conventional act-scene-line references and sometimes without, the inclusion here may assist users of this edition in working their way through secondary materials.

Although the F1 text has been silently modernized, any significant variations in wording are recorded in the notes and speech prefixes have been regularized, usually without notation. I follow the punctuation in F1 so far as that is possible, silently emending when I think a modern reader might be misled. Material, particularly stage directions, that has been editorially added is enclosed in square brackets [ ]. Every spoken line is numbered, but not lines containing act and scene divisions or only stage directions.

I would like to thank Professor George Walton Williams for several helpful suggestions about the text of this play.

William Proctor Williams

On the CD

1. Introduction to the Sourcebooks Shakespeare *Macbeth*: Sir Derek Jacobi

ACT 1, SCENE 1, LINES 1–13

2. Narration: Sir Derek Jacobi
3. Three Witches
   Mercury Theatre • *1940*
4. Three Witches
   Naxos AudioBooks • *1998*

ACT 1, SCENE 3, LINES 38–88

5. Narration: Sir Derek Jacobi
6. Orson Welles as Macbeth and Robert Warrick as Banquo
   Mercury Theatre • *1940*
7. Stephen Dillane as Macbeth and Adam Kotz as Banquo
   Naxos AudioBooks • *1998*

ACT 1, SCENE 5, LINES 1–27

8. Narration: Sir Derek Jacobi
9. Sybil Thorndike as Lady Macbeth
   Naxos AudioBooks—Great Historical Shakespeare Recordings • *1930*

ACT 1, SCENE 5, LINES 35–70

10. Narration: Sir Derek Jacobi
11. Harriet Walter as Lady Macbeth and Hugh Ross as Macbeth
    The Complete Arkangel Shakespeare • *2003*
12. Pamela Brown as Lady Macbeth and Alec Guinness as Macbeth
    The Old Vic • *1953*

ACT 1, SCENE 7, LINES 1–28

13. Narration: Sir Derek Jacobi
14. Simon Russell Beale as Macbeth
    Naxos AudioBooks—Great Speeches and Soliloquies • *1994*
15. Orson Welles as Macbeth
    Mercury Theatre • *1940*

ACT 1, SCENE 7, LINES 28–80

16. Narration: Sir Derek Jacobi
17. Pamela Brown as Lady Macbeth and Alec Guinness as Macbeth
    The Old Vic • *1953*
18. Fay Bainter as Lady Macbeth and Orson Welles as Macbeth
    Mercury Theatre • *1940*

ACT 2, SCENE 1, LINES 34–65

19. Narration: Sir Derek Jacobi
20. Simon Russell Beale as Macbeth
    Naxos AudioBooks—Great Speeches and Soliloquies • *1994*
21. Ben Greet as Macbeth
    Pavilion Records—Great Shakespeareans • *1912*

ACT 2, SCENE 2, LINES 37–76

22. Narration: Sir Derek Jacobi
23. Fay Bainter as Lady Macbeth and Orson Welles as Macbeth
    Mercury Theatre • *1940*
24. Arthur Bourchier as Macbeth
    Naxos AudioBooks—Great Historical Shakespeare Recordings • *1909*

ACT 2, SCENE 3, LINES 1–36

25. Narration: Sir Derek Jacobi
26. David Tennant as the Porter and Gary Bakewell as Macduff
    The Complete Arkangel Shakespeare • *2003*

ACT 3, SCENE 1, LINES 47–71

27. Narration: Sir Derek Jacobi
28. Alec Guinness as Macbeth
    The Old Vic • *1953*
29. Stephen Dillane as Macbeth
    Naxos AudioBooks • *1998*

ACT 4, SCENE 1, LINES 1–38

30. Narration: Sir Derek Jacobi
31. Orson Welles as Macbeth, and the Three Witches
    Mercury Theatre • 1940

ACT 5, SCENE 1, LINES 24–54

32. Narration: Sir Derek Jacobi
33. Pamela Brown as Lady Macbeth
    The Old Vic • 1953
34. Fiona Shaw as Lady Macbeth
    Naxos AudioBooks • 1998

ACT 5, SCENE 5, LINES 17–28

35. Narration: Sir Derek Jacobi
36. Orson Welles as Macbeth
    Mercury Theatre • 1940
37. Stephen Dillane as Macbeth
    Naxos AudioBooks • 1998

ACT 5, SCENE 7, LINES 30–63

38. Narration: Sir Derek Jacobi
39. Hugh Ross as Macbeth and Gary Bakewell as Macduff
    The Complete Arkangel Shakespeare • 2003
40. Orson Welles as Macbeth and George Coulouris as Macduff
    Mercury Theatre • 1940

41. Introduction to Speaking Shakespeare: Sir Derek Jacobi
42. Speaking Shakespeare: Andrew Wade with Drew Cortese

43. Conclusion of the Sourcebooks Shakespeare *Macbeth*: Sir Derek Jacobi

Featured Audio Productions

NAXOS AUDIOBOOKS (1998)

Macbeth	Stephen Dillane
Lady Macbeth	Fiona Shaw
Duncan	Denys Hawthorne
Malcolm/Apparition 2	Declan Conlan
Banquo	Adam Kotz
Macduff/Apparition 1	Colin Tiernay
Ross	Nick Gecks
Lennox	Bruce Alexander
Porter	Bill Paterson
Witch 1	Annette Badland
Witch 2	Joyce Henderson
Witch 3/Gentlewoman	Pauline Lynch
Hecate	June Watson
Doctor/Old Man/Siward	John Rogan
Donalbain/Young Siward	Benjamin Soames
Fleance/Apparition 3	James Boxer
Lady Macduff	Stella Gonet
Son of Macduff	Stephanie Lane
Captain/First Murderer/	
Caithness/Lord/Seyton	David Timson
Second Murderer/Mentheith/	
Servant	Jonathan Keeble
Angus/Servant/Soldier/	
Third Murderer	Peter Yapp

THE OLD VIC PRODUCTION (1953)

Duncan	John Bushelle
Malcolm	Anthony Service
Donalbain	Philip Guard
Macbeth	Alec Guinness
Banquo	Andrew Cruickshank
Macduff	Robin Bailey
Lennox	Stanley van Beers
Ross	Mark Dignam
Mentieth	Gordon Davies
Angus	Geoffrey Wincott
Fleance	Jill Nyasa
Siward	Not named
Seyton	Patric Doonan
Boy, son to Macduff	Gabrielle Blunt
Doctor	Geoffrey Bayldon
Lady Macbeth	Pamela Brown
Lady Macduff	Rachel Gurney
First Witch	Mary O'Farrell
Second Witch	Margaret Vines
Third Witch	Jill Nyasa
First Murderer/Porter	George Rose
Second Murderer	Geoffrey Bayldon
Third Murderer	Patric Doonan
Ghost of Banquo	Gordon Davies
Old Man	Geoffrey Wincott
Servant	Philip Guard
Waiting Gentlewoman	Margaret Vines

THE MERCURY THEATRE PRODUCTION (1940)

Narrator	William Alland
Macbeth	Orson Welles
Lady Macbeth	Fay Bainter
Banquo	Robert Warrick
Duncan	Erskine Sanford
Macduff	George Coulouris
Lady Macduff	Edith Barrett
The Porter	Erskine Sanford
Malcolm	Edgar Barrier
Donalbain	William Alland
Fleance	Sam Edwards
Lennox	Richard Wilson
Ross	Richard Baer
Angus	George Coulouris
Siward	Erskine Sanford
Young Siward	Richard Baer
Seyton	Erskine Sanford
The Doctor	George Coulouris
Gentlewoman	Edith Barrett
Macduff's Son	Sam Edwards

THE COMPLETE ARKANGEL SHAKESPEARE (2003)

Macbeth	Hugh Ross
Lady Macbeth	Harriet Walter
Banquo	John Bowe
Macduff	Gary Bakewell
Malcolm	Mark Bonnar
Duncan	Denys Hawthorne
First Witch	Shirley Dixon
Second Witch	Margaret Robertson
Third Witch	Maureen Beattie
Porter	David Tennant
Ross	Sean Baker
Siward	Gavin Muir
Fleance	Peter England
Old Man	Michael Deacon

Other parts played by: Alasdair Galbraith, Sidney Livingstone, Alex Lowe and Nicholas Murchie

Naxos AudioBooks—Great Historical Shakespeare Recordings
Sybil Thorndike and Lewis Casson as Lady Macbeth and Macbeth (1930)
Arthur Bourchier as Macbeth (1909)

Naxos AudioBooks—Great Speeches and Soliloquies
Simon Russell Beale and Estelle Kohler as Macbeth and Lady Macbeth (1994)

Pavilion Records—Great Shakespeareans
Ben Greet as Macbeth (1912)

Note from the Series Editors

For many of us, our first and only encounter with Shakespeare was in school. We may recall that experience as a struggle, working through dense texts filled with unfamiliar words. However, those of us who were fortunate enough to have seen a play performed have altogether different memories. It may be of an interesting scene or an unusual character, but it is most likely a speech. Often, just hearing part of one instantly transports us to that time and place. "Friends, Romans, countrymen, lend me your ears," "But, soft! What light through yonder window breaks?," "To sleep, perchance to dream," "Tomorrow, and tomorrow, and tomorrow."

The Sourcebooks Shakespeare series is our attempt to use the power of performance to help you experience the play. In it, you will see photographs from various productions, on film and on stage, historical and contemporary, known worldwide or in your community. You may even recognize some actors you don't think of as Shakespearean performers. You will see set drawings, costume designs, and scene edits, all reproduced from original notes. Finally, on the enclosed audio CD, you will hear scenes from the play as performed by some of the most accomplished Shakespeareans of our times. Often, we include multiple interpretations of the same scene, showing you the remarkable richness of the text. Hear Orson Welles in a recording from the 1940s reciting Macbeth's famous soliloquy "Tomorrow, and tomorrow, and tomorrow." Compare that to a contemporary version by Stephen Dillane from 1998. The actors create different worlds, different characters, different meanings.

As you read the text of the play, you can consult explanatory notes for definitions of unfamiliar words and phrases or words whose meanings have changed. These notes appear on the left pages, next to the text of the play. The audio, photographs, and other production artifacts augment the notes and they too are indexed to the appropriate lines. You can use the pictures to see how others have staged a particular scene and get ideas on costumes, scenery, blocking, etc. As for the audio, each track represents a particular interpretation of a scene. Sometimes, a passage that's difficult to comprehend opens up when you hear it out loud. Furthermore, when you hear more than one version, you gain a keener understanding of the characters. Did Lady Macbeth really push Macbeth to murder Duncan or was it Macbeth's own "vaulting ambition"? Would he have acted on his own, without a push from her? The actors made their choices and so can you. You may even come up with your own interpretation.

The text of the play, the definitions, the production notes, the audio—all of these work together, and they are included for your enjoyment. Because the audio consists of performance excerpts, it is meant to entertain. When you see a passage with an associated clip, you can read along as you hear the actors perform the scenes for you. Or, you can sit back, close your eyes, and listen, and then go back and reread the text with a new perspective. Finally, since the text is actually a script, you may find yourself reciting the lines out loud and doing your own performance!

You will undoubtedly notice that some of the audio does not exactly match the text. Also, there are photographs and facsimiles of scenes that aren't in your edition. There are many reasons for this, but foremost among them is the fact that Shakespeare scholarship continues to move forward and the prescribed ways of dealing with and interpreting text are always changing. Thus a play that was edited and published in the 1900s will be different from one published in 2005. Finally, artists have their own interpretation of the play and they too cut and change lines and scenes according to their vision.

The ways in which *Macbeth* has been presented have varied considerably through the years. We've included essays in the book to give you glimpses into the range of the productions, showing you how other artists have approached the play and providing examples of just what changes were made and how. Gregory Doran writes of the 1999 Royal Shakespeare production of *Macbeth* he directed, starring Anthony Sher. He sets the play in a modern, militaristic society, and Sher's interpretation of the title role relied partly on black humor. "In Production," an essay by our text editor, William Proctor Williams, provides an overview of how the play has been performed through the years, from the flying witches resembling vaudevillians in 1664 to Kemble's witches as creatures of doom in 1749 to Orson Welles's "Voodoo" Macbeth in 1936. In "Hours Dreadful and Things Strange," Douglas Lanier cites a myriad of examples of pop appropriations, including ones from music, horror stories, comics, and Gothic novels. He discusses numerous adaptations of the play throughout the world, including productions from China, Japan, India, and Venezuela. Finally, for the actor in you (and for those who want to peek behind the curtain), we have two essays that you may find especially intriguing. Andrew Wade, voice coach of the Royal Shakespeare Company for sixteen years, shares his point of view on how to understand the text and speak it. You can also listen in on him working with an actor on the opening speech of the play; perhaps you too can learn the art of speaking Shakespeare. The last essay is from an interview we conducted: we talked to each member of a cast and asked the actors about their characters and relationships. We found it fascinating to hear what they had to say on various topics; for instance, incorporating the witches as household servants, or Macbeth's inability to father children, possibly causing him to feel the need to constantly prove his manhood. The characters come to life in a way that's different from reading the book or watching a performance.

One last note: we are frequently asked why we didn't include the whole play, either in audio or video. While we enjoy the plays and are avid theatergoers, we are trying to do something more with the audio (and the production notes and the essays) than just presenting them to you. In fact, our goal is to provide you tools that will enable you to explore the play on your own, from many different directions. Our hope is that the different pieces of audio, the voices of the actors, and the old production photos and notes will all engage you and illuminate the play on many levels, so that you can construct your own understanding and create your own "production," a fresh interpretation unique to you.

Though the productions we referenced and the audio clips we have included are but a miniscule sample of the play's history, we hope they encourage you to further delve into the works of Shakespeare. New editions of the play come out yearly; movie adaptations are regularly being produced; there are hundreds of theater groups in the U.S. alone; and performances could be going on right in your backyard. We echo the words of noted writer and poet Robert Graves, who said, "The remarkable thing about Shakespeare is that he is really very good—in spite of all the people who say he is very good."

We welcome you now to The Sourcebooks Shakespeare edition of *Macbeth*.

Dominique Raccah

Marie Macaisa

Dominique Raccah and Marie Macaisa
Series Editors

track 1

Introduction to the Sourcebooks Shakespeare *Macbeth*
Sir Derek Jacobi

William Proctor Williams

Macbeth, the shortest of all of Shakespeare's tragedies and one of the shortest of all his plays, was probably written in 1606 as an elaborate compliment to James I, who had become king of England in 1603 upon the death of Elizabeth I. After all, he had written a book on witches (*Daemonologie, 1597*) and Banquo was one of his legendary ancestors.

The cover of James I's *Daemonologie*
Folger Shakespeare Library

Yet the play has proven to have a universal fascination. It has been viewed as a critique on the philosophy of "the ends justify the means" and on the corrupting power of suggestion (the Witches' prophecies in 1.3 and 4.1).

It has also been seen as an exploration of the relationship between husband and wife as they scramble toward power. It has even been studied as a guide to success or failure in the business world (see Paul Corrigan, *Shakespeare on Management,* London, 1999, and Peter Foster, "Macbarrett and the Bard," *National Post*, February 27, 1999, p. D5).

One aspect of the play that has always attracted considerable interest is the question of ambiguity in language—what we would now likely call "spin." This starts at the very end of the first scene when the Witches exit chanting, "Fair is foul, and foul is fair." Macbeth's first line in the play is, "So foul and fair a day I have not seen" (1.3.38). Even the Porter goes on about equivocation. This notion of double meaning hovers over the play to the very end when Macbeth says:

> and begin
> To doubt the equivocation of the fiend
> That lies like truth. "Fear not till Birnam wood
> Do come to Dunsinane," and now a wood
> Comes toward Dunsinane.

> 5.5.42–5.5.46

Perhaps it is because we all feel that many of the doings of the world are fraught with ambiguity that we are perpetually interested in appearance and reality, word and deed. We are troubled that fair may really be foul. It is "bait and switch" on a cosmic scale.

Macbeth has one of the longest recorded stage histories of any of Shakespeare's plays. Although we believe it was performed at Court before James I in 1606, the earliest documented performance is that attended by Simon Forman at the Globe in the spring of 1611 and described in his diary. As Forman does not mention some striking scenes—the opening with the Witches (1.1), the cauldron scene (4.1), or the prophecies ("man of woman born" and "Birnam Wood coming to Dunsinane")—it is possible that the play at the Globe during this period did not include them. Unfortunately, we do not know nearly as much as we would like to know about how *Macbeth* and other plays were performed at the Globe.

Sir William Davenant produced the next recorded performance of the play on November 5, 1664; the theaters had been closed from 1642–1660 by order of Parliament. Davenant made very substantial changes to both the plot and language, enlarging Lady Macduff's part considerably and making her a foil for Lady Macbeth. He added a scene for Lady Macbeth where she sees Banquo's Ghost, and he turned the Witches into near vaudevillians. Samuel Pepys, the diarist, saw this production several times and on April 14, 1667, he wrote, "So to the playhouse . . . Here we saw 'Macbeth,' which, though I have seen it often, yet it is one of the best plays for a stage, and variety of dancing and music, that ever I saw." John Downes, Davenant's prompter, described the production as "being dressed in all its finery, as new clothes, new scenes, machines as flyings for the Witches; with all the singing and dancing in it . . . being in the nature of an opera . . . it proves still a lasting play." The play's popularity was certainly enhanced by the fact that two of the leading actors of the time, Thomas Betterton and his wife, took the title roles and were much acclaimed—an indication that no matter how much Davenant might have done to the play, the importance of Macbeth and Lady Macbeth was not diminished. Indeed it did prove lasting, since this version of the play held the London stage for eighty years with a succession of the leading actors of their time (Betterton gave his last performance in 1709 at the age of seventy-four, a year before his death). As would be the case throughout the eighteenth century, the production was played in contemporary garb and there was no attempt to dress it as either Scottish or Jacobethan.

In 1744, David Garrick, the undoubted darling of the London stage after his *Hamlet* and *King Lear* of the preceding two years, mounted a production of *Macbeth* that restored most of the text cut by Davenant, though not the porter scene. In addition, Garrick, a consummate showman of his age, gave Macbeth a dying speech. Davenant had Macbeth die on stage and had given him a dying line: "Farewell vain World, and what's most vain in it, Ambition." Garrick's Macbeth also dies on stage with this additional speech:

'Tis done! The scene of life will quickly close.
Ambition's vain, delusive dreams are fled,
And now I wake to darkness, guilt and horror;
I cannot bear it ! Le me shake it off—
It will not be; my soul is clogg'd with blood—

I cannot rise! I dare not ask for mercy—
It is too late, hell drags me down; I sink,
I sink—Oh!—my soul is lost for ever!

Actors can play Macbeth in a number of ways. Garrick chose to play him as a man of moral principles and duty who feels acute guilt for his actions. Typically, such actors are paired with a Lady Macbeth who is a domineering, sometimes very oppressive, character. So it was with Garrick when he finally found Hannah Pritchard, who towered over him in a contemporary painting of Lady Macbeth confronting Macbeth with the daggers at 2.2.50.

David Garrick in the role of Macbeth
Mary Evans Picture Library

But Garrick made little attempt to elaborately dress the stage or interpret the play as a part of Scottish history. That was done by the next important Macbeth, John Philip Kemble. In large part because of the increasing size of theatres (the remodeled Drury Lane could seat three thousand and had the largest stage in Europe at the time), there was an increasing emphasis on large and elaborate sets. For Macbeth, this meant an emphasis on the medieval and Scottish nature of the play, and this extended to costuming. In 1749 Kemble opened the newly enlarged Drury Lane with a production of the play that did away with the dancing and flying of the Witches and turned them into the creatures of doom and fatefulness they have been ever since. Kemble continued the tradition of playing Macbeth as a basically honorable man who is seduced into evil as much by his wife as by the Witches. He was also the first to stage the banquet scene (3.4) without Banquo's Ghost. This was not a popular decision at that time, and he was forced to restore the ghost. However, since then, it has become one of the standard ways of performing the scene.

Perhaps the greatest British Macbeth of the nineteenth century was William Charles Macready, who first performed the part at Covent Garden in 1820. In addition to using the sort of elaborate costumes, sets, tableaux, and processions that audiences had grown to expect, he also professed great concern for the details of the text. He portrayed Macbeth as a complex character who reacted, sometimes almost primitively, to the events he confronted. Performing with various Lady Macbeths for thirty years, it was Macready who brought about a kind of equality between the two and shed the hen-pecked Macbeths of his predecessors. He toured North America several times starting in the mid-1820s, always with great success save for his last visit in 1848–49, when a rivalry with the younger American actor Edwin Forrest, further inflamed by the patriotic press, caused supporters of Forrest to storm the Astor Place Theater in New York. Troops summoned to reinforce the police eventually opened fire on the rioters, killing more than twenty of them. This was the first time in the history of the United States that troops fired on their own citizens. Although this was not the start of the superstition about *Macbeth* being a play associated with bad luck, it certainly did nothing to lessen it.

For the balance of the nineteenth century the play continued to be a star turn for the leading actors of their time, including Sarah Bernhardt and Leon-Hyacinth Marias in a French prose translation that played three times in London in 1884. The stagings became more and more grand so that by 1911, when Herbert Beerbohm Tree staged the play at His Majesty's Theatre in London, he was employing more than one hundred people in the production. The costume and set changes added so much to the running time of the play that in order to keep the performance under four hours, Beerbohm Tree had to cut about one third of the text—this in one of Shakespeare's shortest plays. Performance values were in danger of eclipsing the characters, and even the plot.

Herbert Beerbohm Tree as Macbeth in 1911 staging of *Macbeth*
Mary Evans Picture Library

During this period a strange thing had happened to the Witches. From being a chorus line, as they had been from the Restoration through the eighteenth century, they were gradually transformed into something quite like a dramatic chorus. In addition to their three or four scripted appearances they began to hover over and around many of the other scenes, particularly those involving Macbeth. This use of the non-textual appearances of the Witches has persisted to the present and often serves to enhance the power, or at least the threat, of the supernatural much further than the text will probably bear. This was particularly the case at the turn of the nineteenth century, with the two standard staging methods. While mainline theatre went in for elaborate pictorial settings firmly located in a medieval, though largely fictional, Scotland, starting in the 1890s William Poel began producing Shakespeare on stages which resembled, as closely as possible, those English Renaissance stages that scholars had begun to describe. He staged *Macbeth* in 1909 at the Grand Theatre in Fulham, London. Aside from the replacement of the proscenium arch with a bare thrust stage and the abandonment of any props that could not be carried on and off stage by the actors, he costumed his players in Elizabethan dress and used texts as faithful to their originals as could be managed. Although Poel's innovations influenced many, notably Harley Granville-Barker, and are the first stirrings of the movement towards "authenticity" that would result in the Bankside Globe in London in 1997 and the Blackfriars Playhouse in Staunton, Virginia, in 2001, Poel's productions and those of the mainline theatres had the effect of making the plays seem remote to their audiences. And neither style did anything to lessen the mystery and foreboding surrounding the Witches.

Starting in 1928 with Barry Jackson's production of the play at the Birmingham Repertory Theatre in England, it became common to perform the play in modern dress and with very spare settings. This trend, which has not really yet abated, had the effect of shifting the focus of the play back upon Macbeth and Lady Macbeth and removing the "long-ago-and-far-awayness" of the productions of the preceding century or more. The most prominent of these was John Gielgud's *Macbeth* of 1930 at the Old Vic and of 1942 at the Piccadilly Theatre. Macbeth was depicted not so much as a military hero but as a man tormented by his desire for the crown and his knowledge of what he must do to achieve it.

Arguably the most notable production of *Macbeth* before the Second World War was Orson Welles's "Voodoo" *Macbeth* in 1936 in Harlem. The production was supported by the Federal Theatre Project, part of President Roosevelt's New Deal during the Great Depression. Using an entirely black cast and crew, Welles set the play in a version of Haiti and was able to combine the politics of usurpation with an overwhelming depiction of the supernatural and witchcraft. Enhanced with voodoo dancing and music, his production has not since been equaled. The show, a tremendous success, transferred to Broadway and then toured major cities in the United States as well as London.

Welles revisited *Macbeth* in 1948 when he produced, directed, and starred in his film of the play, which many find to be very idiosyncratic but which continued the themes of political evil and the powers of the supernatural found in the "Voodoo" *Macbeth*.

Orson Welles's 1936 production of "Voodoo" Macbeth
Library of Congress, Music Division, Federal Theatre Project Collection

World War Two not only nearly stopped theatrical productions worldwide, it also changed the way the Macbeths were portrayed and greatly extended the range of new production media, film and video. The general interest in psychoanalysis in the postwar period, coupled with our growing knowledge immediately after the war of the horrors enacted by the Axis powers, affected profoundly the way the two principal characters were played. Productions either concentrated on the mental turmoil of Macbeth, as did Laurence Olivier at Stratford in 1955 and Ian McKellen at the RSC in 1976, or created a brutal military man willing to do anything to achieve his desires, as was the case with Antony Sher at the RSC in 1999, where Sher and the other males in the cast were described as being like "Balkan guerillas." Generally, the supernatural, which had for so long been a regular feature of the play, was less emphasized. Productions such as Peter Hall's at the RSC in 1967, which tried to read the play in Christian terms, used the Weird Sisters almost as adjuncts to the overwhelming evil the Macbeths visit on Scotland. The England scene (4.3), with its references to the saintly King Edward the Confessor's touching to cure the illness of his people, is seen in sharp contrast to what is happening in Scotland.

Ian McKellen as Macbeth in the 1976 RSC production directed by Trevor Nunn
Photo by Donald Cooper

The technological advantages of film and video have had some effect on the performance of *Macbeth*. They allow the display of "stage business" without a huge investment in time and resources. For example, the exiting or vanishing of the Witches can be a simple yet sometimes very telling matter, as in the opening of Roman Polanski's 1971 film where they close the play's first scene by walking away over a beach of wet sand but leave no footprints. Obviously all sorts of tricks can be, and have been, employed in filming the banquet scene (3.4).

However, no matter the medium, the last fifty years have seen the performance of this play continue to focus intensely on the characters of Macbeth and his lady. Indeed, in November of 2005 the BBC broadcast a televised adaptation in which "Joe Macbeth is a head chef in a top restaurant. While the owner Duncan swans from one celebrity party to another garnering praise, Joe is the one putting culinary masterpieces on the tables. Three binmen [garbage men] meet Joe and tell him that the restaurant will win acclaim and that Joe will become its owner. Joe's wife Ella urges Joe to continue his rapid rise. If they kill Duncan, the restaurant for which they've worked so hard will be theirs" (BBC1). The applications of the play do truly seem infinite in their variety.

The play has remained exceedingly popular from 1604 until today. The *World Shakespeare Bibliography Online* records 1,159 performances of some kind somewhere in the world between 1964 and 2005, or about twenty-eight per year, and the Royal Shakespeare Company's archive records sixty-seven productions, tours, or restagings by that company or its predecessors at Stratford-upon-Avon between 1883 and 2004. It is a play whose investigation of personal and political evil, whether from supernatural urgings or internal motives, has become deeply embedded in the consciousness of the English-speaking world, and probably the literate world in general.

As Performed

Gregory Doran

CHEATING EXPECTATION

"Macbeth, Macbeth, Macbeth!" I chanted at the start of our rehearsals. "There, it's said. And I haven't had to leave the room, turn round three times or spit. The so-called curse of Macbeth has nothing to do with some fictitious hex on this play; the curse is that it's a very difficult play to pull off." So I banned superstitious nonsense and refused to hear it referred to as "The Scottish Play." I know of a recent production of *Twelfth Night* in which one actor fell seriously ill, another left with stage fright, and another lost a close relative and had to withdraw, and no one referred darkly to the curse of the "Illyrian play!"

Macbeth begins with the Three Witches, so that's where we began—not with a debate about how to stage the supernatural, but with a discussion about the word that appears most in the play: "fear." I asked the actors to dig deep and share a memory of when they have genuinely experienced fear. The responses were many and varied: fear of the dark, of spiders, of intruders, fear of losing someone, fear of death or danger, fear of failure. No one said fear of ghosts or witches. They described the physical aspects of fear, the physiological effect it had upon the body: the alertness, the breath, the tension. We were ready.

As always, I start rehearsals by reading the play as if the ink were still wet on the page. We read around the table, with no one playing their own parts. Then everyone puts the text into his or her own words. The actor with the smallest role may illuminate a word or line with a fresh insight, and as a consequence, three things happen: 1) our mutual understanding of the play deepens; 2) the sharing of ideas breeds a greater investment in the production; and 3) the company begins to grow into an ensemble.

The first few scenes of the play require detailed examination and precise understanding. Without this rigor, they can plod by in a blur of bloody captains. The director's job is not to have all the right answers but to identify the right questions, to interrogate the text. What exactly is the crisis? What is the threat? Who is the Thane of Cawdor and who the merciless Macdonwald? And why does Macbeth fight the rebel with such fierce energy? The violence of his fighting does not seem to display any of "the milk of human kindness" that his wife is to accuse him of.

And who are the Witches? Throughout the rehearsal period I rehearsed the actresses playing the Witches separately from the rest of the cast. Privately, we referred to them as the "Weird Sisters," the name Shakespeare gives them. Everyone else called them "Witches," a pejorative term. It is not how they think of themselves. We decided they are real women who somehow believe they have the power of foresight. They know that Macbeth will be king but can only tell him if he asks them to speak. They want to tell him: everyone loves imparting good news. Unfortunately they also know that Banquo's children will succeed Macbeth and are thus forced to impart their knowledge to him when he addresses them.

They believe they have magical powers (like flight) that are granted them in exchange for their submission to a malicious external force. They are controlled by it. In turn, it gives them some control in their otherwise powerless lives at the bottom of the social pile. They are used to abuse and are vindictive in response.

Where does their belief come from? Drugs? Mental illness? Sexual frustration? We investigated these in private rehearsal and then would run the scene on the blasted heath with Macbeth and Banquo, without telling the other actors what might happen. So sometimes the girls played the scene as if they were off their heads on some fierce narcotic, as if jibberingly high on cocaine or crack, or ecstatically aroused, or as if hallucinating on marijuana or LSD; sometimes they would play overwhelming sexual frustration, or overpowering need, bursting to tell their secrets. Again we would play them as if they had escaped from their asylum and needed to impart their secrets before the inevitable restraint that would soon occur. And after each experiment we would assess what had and had not worked and ultimately we would blur the distinctions, cover our tracks, so that no one could apply simple explanations: "Oh I see, they are playing the Witches as dropouts."

The most difficult thing in performance is to confound expectation. In the first scene, we decided to keep the audience guessing, and to make them listen, to allow their imagination to work. *Macbeth* takes place in the dark: almost the entire play occurs at night, and if scenes are set during the day, the characters comment on the bad weather or how unusually gloomy it is: "So foul and fair a day I have not seen" or "By th' clock, 'tis day, / And yet dark night strangles the travailing lamp." The daylight in the England scene therefore contributes to a sense of freedom and release from the tyranny, the dark forces of evil. We started our production therefore by plunging the audience into darkness. Total darkness, a darkness we rarely experience in our orange-lit city nights.

Anthony Sher as Macbeth and Harriet Walter as Lady Macbeth entering as king and queen
Photo: Donald Cooper

When the house had settled, the First Witch spoke, but no lights came up. The audience strained to see them, but cheated of light their other senses kicked in: they looked with their ears. At the end, as the sisters imagine their familiars, Graymalkin and Paddock, calling them, they rise up to "hover through the fog and filthy air."

During the previews we actually made this happen in the blackout by suspending three speakers at the actresses' head height and projecting the Witches' voices through them.

The audience imagined that the real people were standing in front of them on stage. Then, as the Witches chant their subversive manifesto "Fair is foul and foul is fair," we winched the speakers over the audience's heads, so that the voices sounded above them in the air. The effect was very weird. Already nervous because of the total blackout, the audience erupted in squeals of surprise, which didn't quite settle for some way into the next scene. I heard my old drama teacher Rudi Shelly wagging his ancient Jewish finger at me and saying in his Prussian drawl, "Greeeeeg, don't want to be clever!" It's the best piece of advice any classical theater director can receive. We cut the effect after a couple of previews.

The appearance of Banquo's Ghost is another startling moment which any creative team has to negotiate. Does he come on or not? Can he magically appear? Is it all in Macbeth's mind? We chose not to bring him on for the first appearance, again to cheat expectation. For the second entrance, when Macbeth has decided he must have been hallucinating and calls for wine, we sent one of the uniformed staff off down stage right. Macbeth held out his goblet, waiting for the servant to return. But Banquo (similarly clad in uniform) came on instead. While Macbeth (and the audience) recovered from the shock, Banquo's Ghost had retreated upstage. The dinner guests hurried down to their host and masked Banquo's departure. By the time Macbeth had followed him, the same servant had returned upstage and Macbeth, thinking he was Banquo, spun him round, only to discover his mistake.

The scene marks Macbeth's descent into genuine madness, and his separation from Lady Macbeth, who is now deeply disturbed at having to witness and try to cover up her husband's mental disintegration. It also marks, of course, her own teetering on the brink of insanity. As the guests are ushered out, the couple slumps in a sort of weary horror. In rehearsal one day, Harriet Walter and Antony Sher as the Macbeths, having experienced the mad hurtle of the banquet scene, reached the moment when Lady Macbeth suggests that they need to get some sleep. The absurdity of the notion that sleep would cure anything or indeed that they could ever enjoy the innocence of slumber ever

Ken Bones as Banquo
Photo: Donald Cooper

again suddenly launched them into a fit of giggles, real horrid laughter. It was an electrifying moment that stayed in performance.

As Macbeth leaves, Harriet wanted Lady Macbeth to take a candle from the dining table to light her way, a brilliant notion that would prefigure the sleepwalking scene. She already needs light by her; the dark is too filled with dangerous shadows. I decided to mark this moment of paranoia and push it further. As she left the room she hesitated as if she had heard something, turned round to look, and then retreated. As she did so, all the candles on the table suddenly extinguished themselves.

Harriet's idea had coincided with my own thoughts about how to affect the transition into the next scene, the "witches' cavern," which starts with probably the most difficult (and potentially risible) text in the play: the "double-double" chanting as the sisters toss a lot of animal parts into the cauldron; a chant every Halloween witch has clichéd into parody. What is the props department to provide for the eye of newt, or more ridiculously, the toe of frog? We had already replaced the pilot's thumb in the first act with a rusty nail; were we to think up similar substitutions for the finger of the birth-strangled babe?

In the end, our solution was to apply our rule of cheating the audience's expectations. The sudden extinguishing of the candles on the Macbeth's dinner table was followed by a match being struck under the table, and then another and another. In multiple shadows on the white damask tablecloth, the Witches appeared in frenzied occupation. They had been there all the time, through the banquet, under the table. In the flickering light, they tore and picked at imaginary objects while chanting obsessively their overfamiliar recipe. As Macbeth then appeared in search of them, they suddenly erupted from under the table, tipping the contents of the table all over the floor in a cascade of shattering crockery.

The so-called cavern scene calls directly for chilling effects as the sisters make various apparitions arise. So how should the apparitions appear? Are they all in Macbeth's mind? And if they do appear, do they run the risk of seeming absurd?

Our stage setting for the play, from the very start, was deceptively simple. This was a deliberate choice, with the apparition scene ultimately in mind. As the audiences arrived, they imagined they were sitting in the familiar wooden galleried Swan Theatre that many of them knew well. The stage was bare and there seemed to be no set. In fact we had brought the back wall forward, and an entire fake wall, modeled on the Victorian walls of the Swan, filled the proscenium line. Sections of the wall were made of the same rubberized material that wet suits are made from, and painted to resemble plaster and brick. So when the weird sisters summoned up the apparitions, actors behind the wall could push their faces and upper torsos into the fabric and for a few seconds it seemed as if the solid walls of the theater themselves had erupted into howling life. This wall was later pulled back in a blackout and suddenly and shockingly replaced with an entire forest of handheld trees for Birnam wood. The very walls of Dunsinane seemed to have melted in revolt at Macbeth's evil.

In the end the success of the play does not or should not rely on the "effects." Of course. Much more important in creating the tension of this extraordinary play is the quality of the acting.

The famous theater director of the forties and fifties Tyrone Guthrie said that 80 percent of good directing is good casting. I agree with him. As I've said, I had Harriet Walter and Antony Sher as the Macbeths. We did not proceed until both of them had agreed to do the play. I knew Jo O'Connor would bring to Duncan precisely that air of dignity bordering on sanctity that allows Duncan's murder to be not just an assassination but a sacrilege. Ken Bones would apply a wolfish appetite to Banquo that would match Macbeth's. Nigel Cooke approached me himself, determined to play the part of Macduff. His blazing integrity as an actor and the intensity of his principles as a man allowed him to present Macduff's unswerving lack of compromise without sentimentality.

But I had also learned an important lesson from RSC Honorary Director John Barton, who told me that since the lead actors can generally take care of themselves, my attention must be directed towards all the other parts and in particular, to the smaller parts. So, what, for example, should one do with the Porter?

You can drown in options. I had a very brilliant young actor, Steve Noonan, a skilled mimic with an anarchic streak and flair for improvisation. Just the sort of clown Hamlet would have fretted about. We concluded that the Porter needs to explode into the play with the shock of a bursting balloon, deflating the tension while at the same time intensifying it.

We also agreed that the political topicality of the references to farmers, and particularly equivocators, was extremely hard to get across. I allowed Steve a degree of license, and soon the equivocating voice of the politician hedging his bets became an impersonation of Tony Blair. His rapport with the audience was dangerously fascinating. On the line "What are you?" he would ask a member of the audience for their profession, and then riff on the answer. The nights he happened to solicit a teacher or a psychiatrist were particularly fruitful. On one occasion he chanced upon the Secretary of State for the Foreign Office and all hell was let loose. One lady objected, and the moment became Pirandellian:

"Is this in the play?" she demanded.

"Well, I'm in the play," Steve returned.

But back to the leading couple. Working with actors of the caliber of Harriet Walter and Antony Sher is a genuine thrill. They bring so much to the table: a long experience of working on Shakespeare, a precise analysis of character, an innate sense of rhythm, and a sharply attuned "bullshit meter."

This "bullshit meter" refuses to accept anything untruthful either within my direction or from what their fellow actors might produce.

In order to heighten the danger and tension of the dagger scene where Macbeth returns from the murder of King Duncan with the bloody daggers still in his hand, I had a pair of real daggers brought into rehearsal. They were razor-sharp and could easily slice into flesh. And just to intensify the "reality" of the murder, we added some pig's blood from the local butcher to cover Macbeth's hands. The combination of the very real danger from slipping with the daggers and the genuine revulsion at the warm blood gave the scene an edge of horror that they both carried through into performance.

Harriet Walter as Lady Macbeth and Anthony Sher as Macbeth with the bloody daggers used in Duncan's murder
Photo: Donald Cooper

When Macbeth hears news of his wife's death, he is tilted into an abysmal nihilism. At this point, Shakespeare does a most extraordinary thing. He has Macbeth compare life to an actor "that struts and frets his hour upon the stage," reminding the audience that they are only watching a play. It alerts them of the artificiality of the experience and, at the same time, intensifies that experience by reaffirming their willing complicity in the act of theater taking place. Antony Sher heightened the shock of this by walking off the stage in rehearsal one day, leaving the messenger who subsequently runs on stranded and uncertain what to do. We kept it in, and in each performance, the audience was left unsure of whether the actor or the character had given up. Those little electric shocks can be very potent. Too often the familiarity of Shakespeare text can lead to generality. We have to be alert to its shock, to its strangeness.

So many of the most startling moments of the production came from these actors' intelligent alertness to the opportunities of the text in rehearsal. For example, in the final fight between Macduff and Macbeth, Sher's imagination created a real coup when he suddenly saw Macduff's dagger in the air above him, ready for the fatal stroke. He froze with astonishment. So that was what that weird vision had meant: the dagger that had led him to Duncan's chamber was now to plunge into his heart and end his life.

So I come to the end of the play. Actors ask basic questions that can lead to the most incisive insights. Such a question solved for me the final beat of our production. Someone asked, very simply. "What happens to Fleance?" The Witches' apparitions tell Macbeth that Banquo's offspring will be kings. But in the last scene, Malcolm has reclaimed his rightful position as Duncan's nominated successor. Other productions have had Donalbain hovering in the wings, in sinister anticipation of his turn, but surely Fleance, once he escaped the murderous thugs who dispatch his father, might have been alerted to his destiny by the Weird Sisters? As Malcolm gave his maiden speech as Scotland's new ruler, we had Fleance appear, watching quietly. Perhaps all this is going to happen again?

"Hours Dreadful and Things Strange"

Macbeth IN POPULAR CULTURE

Douglas Lanier

Macbeth AND THE GOTHIC

For contemporary audiences, *Macbeth* is inseparable from the motifs and themes of the Gothic novel and its various mass-media reincarnations, many of which may be traceable to Shakespeare's play. Midnight horrors at an isolated castle, a primal crime that plagues its perpetrator and leads to a series of follow-up crimes, mysterious supernatural events that may or may not be hallucinatory, equivocal prophecies and ironic twists of inescapable fate, an increasing confusion between physical settings and the psychological landscape of the guilty mind—all are recurrent elements of popular Gothic literature that have their direct or indirect origins, or at least strong analogues, in *Macbeth*. Edgar Allan Poe's "The Telltale Heart," to take a very familiar example, shares with Shakespeare's play the murder of a superior by an underling told from the murderer's point of view, intimations of a curse (in the form of the old man's evil eye), covering over of the murder, and the onset of hallucination and madness induced by the killer's guilt.

Modern popular culture offers a number of variations on the basic scenario of *Macbeth* in those modern inheritors of the Gothic form, horror and detective fiction. Such works often toy with the audience's familiarity with the original's plotline. For example, "Fire Burn and Cauldron Bubble," a story in the classic horror comic *Adventures into Terror* 27 (1954), retells the saga of Macbeth with an emphasis on his growing arrogance and cruelty, all springing from his overinvestment in the Witches' prophecies. In the final frame of this adaptation, Macbeth, secure in the knowledge he can be killed only by one "not of woman born," is confronted not by Macduff but by the corpse-like son of one of the Witches, who has used Macbeth's trust in her conjuring to engineer his fall. A freer variation is offered in "Banquo's Chair," a much-beloved American radio show first broadcast on *Suspense*, June 1, 1943. Sir William Brent, a relentless detective, is determined to wrest a confession from John Bedford, a clever, remorseless man who murdered his aunt yet was never convicted of the crime. Brent invites Bedford to a dinner party, and in their midst appears Bedford's dead aunt, visible apparently only to him. Unbeknownst to all but the murderer, Brent has hired an actress to portray the aunt, and the other guests have been instructed beforehand not to acknowledge her presence. That is, to prompt Bedford's confession, Brent slyly restages the confrontation between Macbeth and Banquo's Ghost, a ploy that works exactly as planned to trap the killer. The twist comes at the end, when it is revealed that the actress Brent employed was delayed by bad weather and never arrived. When this work was presented as an episode of the TV series *Alfred Hitchcock Presents!* in 1959, Alfred Hitchcock himself directed.

The association of *Macbeth* with modern Gothic extends beyond the variations offered by horror and detective stories. A Dungeons and Dragons scenario authored by Mark Selinker, "Dark Thane Macbeth," uses Shakespeare's play as its basic foundation. Heavy metal and Goth rock have found Macbeth's defiant rebellion, bloodiness, and inescapable damnation an amenable resource for dark songs about teen angst. Allusions to the play can be found in the songs of such groups as And Also the Trees, Black League, God Machine, Metallica, Sonic Youth, Vader, and an Italian heavy metal band tellingly named Macbeth, as well as such mainstream musicians as Elvis Costello, Indigo Girls, John Cale, and Marianne Faithful. Concept albums by Jag Panzer (*Thane to the Throne*, 2000), Rebellion (*Macbeth: A Tragedy in Steel*, 2002), and Lana Lane (*Lady Macbeth*, 2005) offer full-length heavy metal adaptations of *Macbeth* (Lana Lane's from Lady Macbeth's point of view), and 2006 saw the premiere of a Japanese heavy metal adaptation, *Metaru Makubesu*, by the theater troupe Shinkansen, set in the 1980s and in a dystopian future.

THE CURSE OF "THE SCOTTISH PLAY"
The atmosphere of transgression and doom extends beyond the playscript of *Macbeth* itself to its very staging, for, theatrical tradition would have it, productions of the play are plagued with misfortune. The reigning myth is that

in revenge for Shakespeare's inclusion of magic rituals in the Witches' scenes, actual witches of his day placed a curse on the play. Thereafter, stagings have encountered mysterious accidents, deaths, and disastrous critical reviews. The list of disasters that have befallen productions of *Macbeth* listed in Richard Huggett's *Supernatural on Stage* (1975) is indeed extraordinary. The curse extends, according to popular myth, even to the opening production of the play, where Shakespeare was forced to take the part of Lady Macbeth when the boy playing the role suddenly became feverish (in some versions of the story, it is lead tragedian Richard Burbage who falls ill). Theater folk stress that even uttering the name "Macbeth" in a theater invites bad luck and requires elaborate exorcism rituals, one involving Hamlet's first address to his father's ghost. To avoid invoking the curse, they typically use euphemisms like "The Scottish Play" or "The Comedy of Glamis."

This myth has become a staple of detective or horror stories set in theaters or involving actors. One recurrent plotline concerns a murder or suspicious accident during a production of *Macbeth* that the actors attribute to the famous curse. Upon further investigation a detective discovers that the curse is being used as a cover by the murderer for nefarious activities. Versions of this plotline underlie, to name but a few examples, an episode of the TV show *Columbo* entitled "Dagger of the Mind" (1972), Batman adventures entitled "The Stage Is Set for Murder" (in *Detective Comics* 425, 1972) and "Acts" (in *Batman: Gotham Adventures*, 2001), Dario Argento's horror film *Opera* (1987), Peter Fieldson's play *Stage Fright* (1988), and mystery novels by Marvin Kaye (*Bullets for Macbeth*, 1976), Ngaio Marsh (her superb *Light Thickens*, 1982), Simon Brett (*What Bloody Man Is That?* 1987), William Palmer (*The Detective and Mr. Dickens*, 1990, with Wilkie Collins and Charles Dickens as sleuths), James Yaffe (*Mom Doth Murder Sleep*, 1991), and Stephen Philip Jones (*King of Harlem*, 2001, set during Orson Welles's famous 1936 "Voodoo" production of *Macbeth*). John O'Connor's *Macbeth and the Rebels' Plot* (2001) uses a similar device. His play for children, set in the midst of *Macbeth*'s first production, revolves around the mysterious death of a boy actor.

Equally well represented are stories of *Macbeth* productions that go comically awry because of the curse or, just as often, the ineptitude of the amateur cast. Because such tales celebrate the joys of amateur stage production even as they lampoon it, these narratives often take the form of plays.

Examples include David McGillivray and Walter Zerlin Jr.'s *The Farndale Avenue Housing Estate Townswomen's Guild Dramatic Society's Production of Macbeth* (1983), John Christopher-Wood's *Elsie and Norm's "Macbeth": A Comedy* (1986, later revised to a downtown Glasgow setting), and Eric Brandenburg's *The Lake Wanaga Macbeth* (1997). Student productions of *Macbeth* are also often portrayed as being plagued by comic catastrophes. "Out Darn Spotlight!," a recent episode of the cartoon *The Adventures of Jimmy Neutron, Boy Genius* (2004), depicts just such a student production, as does a short Shakespearean vignette in the teen film *Porky's II* (1983) in which Macduff battles Macbeth with the leg of a manikin. Robert Walker's children's play *Macbeth on the Loose* (2002) depicts a student production comically derailed by jealousies and plotting among cast members that mirror Shakespeare's plot; the idea that life mimics theatrical art, a favorite theme of popular Shakespeare adaptations, is treated with far more seriousness in Greg Lombardo's film *Macbeth in Manhattan* (1999).

THE INFERNAL WOMEN OF *Macbeth*

As the architects of Macbeth's fate, wielders of supernatural powers, and powerful women, the Witches of *Macbeth* have held a special fascination for popular audiences. Interest in their perspective on the play's action, for example, sustains Rebecca Reisert's novel *The Third Witch* (2001), which retells the narrative of *Macbeth* from the Witches' self-justifying perspective. More often in popular culture, however, the Three Witches have taken on a life of their own outside the confines of Shakespeare's play. Their simmering cauldron and line "double, double, toil and trouble" have become culturally commonplace, recognizable enough to be regularly used in advertisements and parodies. Sometimes they serve as a sardonic chorus in horror or fantasy comics, as they do in the opening story of *The Dark Horse Book of Witchcraft* (2004). Terry Pratchett makes the Three Witches—in his book named Granny Weatherwax, Nanny Ogg, and Magrat Garlick—the comic heroes of his much-beloved fantasy novel *Wyrd Sisters* (1980). In Pratchett's reimagining of *Macbeth*, the good king Verence is treacherously murdered by Duke Felmet, and the care of Verence's son, the rightful heir, falls to the Witches, who place him with an acting troupe and plot Felmet's comeuppance; the novel's comic denouement partakes not only of *Macbeth* but also of the play-within-a-play scene from *Hamlet*. His Witches were sufficiently popular to figure in several others of Pratchett's Discworld novels.

Welwyn Wilton Katz's young adult novel *Come Like Shadows* (1993) gives the Witches a far more sinister role. Combining the plotline of the cursed *Macbeth* production with a revisionary interpretation of Macbeth's character (and adding commentary on contemporary Canadian politics to boot), the novel tells the tale of Kinny, a young woman serving as a student intern for a production of *Macbeth* in Stratford, Ontario. In the midst of rehearsals Kinny discovers a magical mirror in which the spirits of Macbeth and the First Witch have been captured. The Witches, she learns, have ruined the reputation of Macbeth and used their charms to seek immortality by targeting someone in the present for possession—herself. Also using the *Macbeth* production narrative and witches with genuine magical powers is Kate Gilmore's young adult novel *Enter Three Witches* (1990). In it, Bren, a boy in a production of *Macbeth,* adjusting to a new girlfriend and coping with his parents' separation, endures the meddling of his mother, grandmother, and neighbor, all of whom are practicing witches and offer their magical help in comically inappropriate ways.

Though Shakespeare describes his Witches as bearded, "filthy hags," several writers have reimagined the trio as young and nubile, their power as much erotic as magical. R. H. E. Crawford's mystery *The Misadventure of the Witches Three* (1997) intersperses the well-worn plotline of a mystery set amidst a troubled local production of *Macbeth* with detective Harold Hudson's sexual romps with three young witches, one of whom has become implicated in the mysterious death of the play's star. Crawford owes much of his reconception of the Witches to John Updike's *The Witches of Eastwick* (1984), a work that uses Shakespeare's Witches as the inspiration for a study of the ambivalent effects of feminist sexual self-empowerment on the battle between men and women. Though Updike's novel doesn't closely parallel Shakespeare's play, the Three Witches do cast a spell to take revenge upon someone they'd formerly embraced, in this case Darryl van Horne, aka Satan himself. And, on a lighter note, in "A Witch's Tangled Hare" (1959), Bugs Bunny battles to avoid becoming an ingredient in the cauldron of Witch Hazel. As they trade tricks in Macbeth's castle, Shakespeare looks on and takes notes, setting up for the climax one of the worst puns in cartoon history.

Though she has had a somewhat more limited afterlife outside Shakespeare's text than the Three Witches, popular culture has been equally fascinated with Lady Macbeth, so much so that her name has become a byword for any ambitious or cold-blooded woman. In the radio play "Lady Macbeth at the Zoo" (1982), for example, the "Lady Macbeth" of the title is a woman plotting murder who is overheard by apes at a zoo. So too is the connotation of the Shakespearean title of Nikolai Leskov's classic novella *Lady Macbeth of Mtsensk* (1865). In it, Katerina, an oppressed wife, plots to murder her husband so that she can pursue a relationship with the family's callow steward, Sergei. This tale of passion and murder in rural pre-Soviet Russia became the basis of two remarkable works, Dmitri Shostakovich's 1934 opera *Lady Macbeth of Mtsensk* (later reworked and renamed *Katerina Ismailova*) and Andrej Wadja's 1962 film *Fury Is a Woman* (aka *A Siberian Lady Macbeth*). By emphasizing Katerina's rebellion against stultifying oppression, Shostakovich and Wajda, both working under oppressive regimes, lent the material a covert but unmistakably subversive political subtext.

Considering Lady Macbeth's reputation for heartlessness and Machiavellianism, it is perhaps not surprising that several popular works seek to rehabilitate her character. Historical novels by Bonnie Copeland (*Lady of Moray,* 1979) and Robert DeMaria (*Stone of Destiny,* 2001) offer revisionary versions of Shakespeare's narrative, while plays by Rob John (*Living with Lady Macbeth,* 1992) and Susan Todd (*The Weird Sisters, Hand in Hand,* 2005) reimagine the play from a feminist perspective. Rae Shirley's play *The Merry Regiment of Women* (1993) also explores Lady Macbeth's potential as a feminist icon; in it, she convenes a meeting of Shakespeare's female characters to protest their discriminatory treatment in the playwright's works. A notable trend in recent productions of *Macbeth* is the sexualization of Lady Macbeth—the extent to which the power she exerts over her husband is erotic. This trend can be seen, for example, in Roman Polanski's treatment of Lady Macbeth in his violent 1971 film adaptation. The sexualization of Lady Macbeth has spawned not only several pornographic film versions but also Jean Binnie's play *Lady Macbeth* (1996), in which the title character uses her power to seduce not only her husband but Macduff as well. It is striking that Japanese culture has found Lady Macbeth so compelling a character and has built adaptations around her. Isoda Aki's one-woman show

Lady Macbeth (1983) and Shozo Sato and Karen Sunde's *Kabuki Lady Macbeth* (2005) have transposed her story into the idioms of Japanese theater, and one of the most memorable characters of Akira Kurosawa's masterful film adaptation *Throne of Blood* (1957) is Lady Macbeth's counterpart, the chillingly steely Lady Asaji.

SAMURAI AND GANGSTERS

Courtney Lehmann has recently observed that many contemporary adaptations of *Macbeth* have minimized or altogether left behind the play's Scottishness. There are a few exceptions to this trend: Jeremy Freeston's 1997 film adaptation firmly locates the action in medieval (and very muddy) Scotland, and the historical record has been the basis of several novelizations, among them Juliet Dymoke's *Shadows on a Throne* (1976), Nigel Tranter's *Macbeth the King* (1978), and Dorothy Dunnett's *King Hereafter* (1982) and subsequent installments in her Lymond Chronicles series. However, like many other Shakespeare plays, *Macbeth* has been transposed to a number of different time periods and settings. Orson

Jack Carter as Macbeth and Edna Thomas as Lady Macbeth in the 1936 production at the New Lafayette Theatre, directed by Orson Welles
Library of Congress, Music Division, Federal Theatre Project Collection

Welles's justly famous 1936 production with an all-black cast (now known as the "Voodoo" *Macbeth*), for example, reset the play in revolutionary Haiti and pursued analogies between Shakespeare's play, voodoo magic, and volatile Caribbean politics. More recently, the drive to resituate Shakespeare's plays in youth culture settings has prompted such works as Neil Arksey's young adult novel *MacB* (1999), which transposes the narrative to the world of high school soccer, and the German film *Rave Macbeth* (dir. Klaus Knoesel, 2001), which reimagines the plot as a fight for drug-dealing supremacy in a trendy dance club.

Isuzu Yamada as Lady Asaji Washizu in Akira Kurosawa's 1957 adaptation, *Throne of Blood (Kumonosu jō)*
Courtesy: Douglas Lanier

A few genres have been perennially attractive to adapters interested in finding analogies for the hierarchical organization of Macbeth's feudal Scotland and its bloody, warlike culture. Akira Kurosawa's much-praised film *Throne of Blood*, for example, recasts Shakespeare's play in terms of the Samurai epic, an approach which Kurosawa blends with elements of

Japanese Noh drama. The constrained intensity of Kurosawa's actors and his talent for painterly images enhance the themes of his source text; Washizu's fumbling for direction in the fog after hearing the prophecy of his rise to power from an eerie spinster ghost, and his terrified death in a climactic hail of arrows, offer powerful visual metaphors for Macbeth's entrapment by a fate he doesn't fully understand. The recent futuristic manga version illustrated by Tony Leonard Tamai (2005) updates the Samurai-inflected *Macbeth* tradition for a new generation.

A number of filmmakers have pursued analogies between Shakespeare's play and mob and crime drama. *Joe Macbeth* (dir. Ken Hughes, 1955) re-envisions the play in terms of *film noir* and gangster film motifs, recasting Macbeth as a mob underling, his wife as a viperous *femme fatale,* and the Witches as a nightclub fortune teller. Though this little-seen film has often been cited by film critics as the nadir of Shakespearean film adaptation, the final scenes in which Joe Macbeth meets his fate in his darkened, echoing mansion are genuinely compelling. More faithful to Shakespeare's plot, *Men of Respect* (dir. William Reilly, 1991) updates the gangster *Macbeth* film by taking up the mood, visual motifs, and even actors from Francis Ford Coppola's *The Godfather* series and Martin Scorsese's gritty New York mob dramas. John Turturro's performance as Mike Battaglia, the counterpart of Macbeth, stresses the character's conflicted ambition and growing sense of doom. Recent films have offered variations on this approach. Two direct-to-video films, *Mad Dawg* (dir. Greg Salman, 2001) and *Bloody Streetz* (dir. Gerald Barclay, 2003), transpose *Macbeth* to black "gangsta" culture, the latter juxtaposing its bloody hero with African immigrants who lament his criminal lifestyle. Penny Woolcock's well-acted TV adaptation *Macbeth on the Estate* (1997) sets the action in a crime-ridden London housing estate. The extraordinary Bollywood crime epic *Maqbool* (dir. Vishal Bhardwaj, 2004) deftly dovetails a story of doomed forbidden love between Maqbool and his mob boss's mistress Nimmi with elements of the *Macbeth* narrative. In it, the Witches' roles are taken up by two comically corrupt cops who cast horoscopes and manipulate lives to maintain a balance between criminal powers; the film's dreamlike handling of the boss's murder provides one of the most memorable moments in recent Shakespearean film. This tradition remains very much alive. As of this writing, Geoffrey Wright's *Macbeth,* a film adaptation of the play reset in the world of Australian gang warfare, is in post-production.

MOCKING *Mac*

Perhaps because it is so familiar and perhaps because its relentless seriousness invites irreverence, *Macbeth* has been a popular choice for parody. The range of comic targets is very broad. Barbara Garson's screed against Lyndon B. Johnson's administration and the Vietnam War, the Shakespearean pastiche *Macbird!* (1965), inaugurated a tradition of using *Macbeth* as a vehicle for political lampoon. In 1998 R. Louis Oueinaught (a pseudonym) produced *MacClintonlet,* a comic view of the Lewinsky scandal and Starr investigation, and coverage thereof by the press, in the style of Garson's *Macbird!*; almost inevitably, Michael Hettinger's *Macbush* followed in 2003. Ric Miller has fashioned a tour-de-force one-man show, *MacHomer* (1996), which cleverly casts characters from *The Simpsons* in a version of Shakespeare's narrative and yields such gems as "Is this a pizza I see before me?" Amazingly, Miller does all the voices. *Macbeth*'s potential for comic treatment has also been exploited in films such as Mackenlay Polhemus's *The Scottish Tale* (1997), which recasts Shakespeare's play as a romantic comedy, and Alison LiCalsi's *Macbeth: The Comedy* (2001), which reimagines the Macbeths as a lesbian couple and the Witches as three gay men.

Curiously, many *Macbeth* lampoons target the kinds of adaptational approaches detailed in this article. The connection between *Macbeth* and detective fiction, for example, is the subject of James Thurber's classic essay "The Macbeth Murder Mystery" (1942), in which the narrator, having read too many mystery novels, tries to solve the enigma of who really killed King Duncan; Tom Stoppard's short play *Cahoot's Macbeth* (1979) inserts a clueless inspector into the play's action. The theme of life imitating art and the curse upon productions of *Macbeth* form the kernel of *500 Clown Macbeth* (2000), in which three clowns vying over the lead role escalate into ever-greater levels of destructiveness, eventually dooming the production. Daisan Erotica, a Japanese theatrical troupe, targets the connections between *Macbeth* and gangsters in its *A Man Called Macbeth* (1997), a play which imagines one of Shakespeare's descendants directing a staging of *Macbeth* using yakuza, Japanese mobsters. And the trend to adapt Shakespeare to contemporary youth culture is skewered in Billy Morrissette's clever slacker film *Scotland, PA* (2001). In it, the Macbeths are twentysomething workers in a rural hamburger joint who murder their boss and invent the modern fast-food restaurant, prompted by hippie witches—one of whom makes her predictions from a Magic 8-Ball. All the while, they are pursued by the dogged Lieutenant Macduff, a vegetarian detective, itself a send-up of the *Macbeth*-detective connection. As several critics have noted, *Scotland, PA* slyly lampoons the "Macdonaldization" of Shakespeare that many have argued was an effect of the teen-film adaptations of Shakespeare that dominated the late 1990s.

GLAMIS GOES GLOBAL

The globalization of Shakespeare has yielded *Macbeth* adaptations in a wide range of cultural contexts, with Far Eastern and African cultures particularly well represented. Perhaps as a result of its long contact with the British Empire, India has produced many adaptations of *Macbeth*. The film *Jwala* (dir. Master Vinayak, 1938) provides an early example of the blending of Shakespearean narrative with indigenous myth. It tells the story of Angar, an Indian general who kills his king after being corrupted by a witch's prophecy of his rise to power; in this version, his wife and compatriot are horrified by his actions and join forces against him. Numerous Indian stage productions have sought to adapt the play to native traditions. To name but two of many: Lokendra Arambam's *Macbeth: Stage of Blood* (1997) used innovative staging and a reverse chronology (the story is told backwards) to meld the play with the culture of Manipur, a northern Indian province; *The Kathakali Macbeth* (2001) uses the traditional southern Indian dance form to tell the story. The Mauritian playwright Dev Virahsawmy has twice adapted *Macbeth* to his native language, first in 1981 (*Zeneral Makbef* [*General McBeef*]) and again in 1997 (*Trazedji Makbess*); his countryman, the novelist Yacoob Ghanty, used *Macbeth* as the architecture for his study of a civil servant's murder of his family in the play *Macbeth Revisited* (1995). Two remarkable adaptations from Africa explore the play's affinities with traditional African cultures. Welcome Msomi's much-produced *Umabatha: The Zulu Macbeth* (1969) resituates the action in the bloody conflicts between rival tribes in nineteenth-century Africa, and its liberal use of traditional dance and music celebrates African heritage. Alexander Abela's modest but affecting film *Makibefo* (2000) sets his adaptation among the poor fishermen of Madagascar and is noteworthy for his use of untrained actors.

Macbeth AROUND THE WORLD

Lokendra Arambam's *Macbeth: Stage of Blood* (1997)—India	innovative staging and reverse chronology
Umabatha: The Zulu Macbeth (1969)—Africa	bloody conflicts between rival tribes in nineteenth-century Africa
Zheng Shifeng's *The Kunju Macbeth: Blood-Stained Hands* (1987)—China	traditional Chinese opera
Zen Zen Zo's Butoh *Macbeth* (1995)—Japan	Japanese avant-garde dance
Leonardo Henríquez's film *Macbeth-Sangrador* (1999)—Latin America	*El Topo* cinematic tradition

China and Japan have also produced versions of *Macbeth* that adapt Shakespeare's plot to native theatrical forms. Zheng Shifeng's *The Kunju Macbeth: Blood-Stained Hands* (1987) and Lee Huei-min's *The Kingdom of Desire* (1990), for example, handle *Macbeth* as traditional Chinese operas. But not all Far Eastern adaptations emphasize such traditionalism. The Japanese avant-garde dance form known as "Butoh," a form that emphasizes the grotesque, expressionistic, and surreal, has twice been the basis for adaptations of *Macbeth*, one by the multinational performance troupe Zen Zen Zo in 1995, and another by American playwright S. Glenn Brown and choreographer Jerry Gardner in 2001. The politics of translation from culture to culture are particularly on display with Michel Garneau's translation of the play into Québecois in 1978. In it, Garneau sought to assert the cultural identity of the language as well as to transform *Macbeth* into an allegory of the province's pursuit of independence. And, finally, Venezuelan director Leonardo Henríquez's film *Macbeth-Sangrador* (1999) brings Shakespeare's play into contact with the bloody and often surreal imagery of the Latin American *El Topo* cinematic tradition. The vitality of *Macbeth*'s adaptation to so many cultural traditions suggests that Shakespeare's tale of dynastic struggles in medieval Scotland has now become a global parable about the temptations and self-destructiveness of ambition and violence, one that continues to find resonance with audiences worldwide.

Dramatis Personae

Three Witches, the Weird Sisters

DUNCAN, King of Scotland

His sons:
MALCOLM
DONALBAIN

MACBETH, Thane of Glamis
LADY MACBETH
SEYTON, Servant to Macbeth
Three Murderers, serving Macbeth

A Doctor
A Gentlewoman
A Porter

BANQUO, a noble and officer in Duncan's army
FLEANCE, his son

MACDUFF, A Scottish lord
LADY MACDUFF
Their Son

Scottish Lords:
LENNOX
ROSS
ANGUS
MENTEITH
CAITHNESS

SIWARD, Earl of Northumberland and commander of the English army
YOUNG SIWARD, his son

A Sergeant in Duncan's army

continued on next page

OLD MAN

A Doctor in the English court

HECATE

APPARITIONS

Lords, Attendants, Servants, Messengers

[Macbeth

Act 1

0: Location: an open place, often described as in "a desert place"

0: Stage Direction: The thunder and lightning was originally produced using either a shaken sheet of metal (thunder sheet) or cannonball rolled down a wooden ramp and the tossing of fireworks from above the stage.

0: Scene: The three witches have been variously portrayed, but not usually in the way one might find in fairy tales. Banquo mentions they have beards, so facial hair has often been made prominent. The 1982–83 RSC production cast them as an ethnically diverse rock group (white, black, and Asian, and with a band) who sang or chanted their lines. A tradition of portraying the third witch as being younger than the other two and often mentally and/or physically impaired has grown (see Polanski's film [1971]). There is nothing in the text that demands that they be women, though they usually are, but in at least one production, they were played by men depicting Nordic gods (Schiller and Goethe, Weimar, 1800).

1–13:
Three Witches from the Mercury Theatre production (1940)
Three Witches from the Naxos AudioBooks production (1998)

tracks 2-4

3: **hurly-burly:** turmoil

9: **Graymalkin:** a common name for a cat and also the First Witch's familiar (a spirit, often embodied in an animal, that serves or guards a person)

10: **Paddock:** a toad and also the Second Witch's familiar

11: **Anon:** immediately

13: Stage Direction: The exit of the witches, like their entry, has been handled a number of ways. In 1888 in Henry Irving's production, they flew off at the end, though they were merely revealed at the opening of the scene. In the early theater, they probably entered and exited from a trap. Film allows even more scope; in Polanski's film, they exit across the sands of the beach, leaving no footprints.

Act 1, Scene 1]

Thunder and lightning
Enter three WITCHES

FIRST WITCH
    When shall we three meet again?
    In thunder, lightning, or in rain?

SECOND WITCH
    When the hurly-burly's done,
    When the battle's lost and won.

THIRD WITCH
    That will be ere the set of sun.   5

FIRST WITCH
    Where the place?

SECOND WITCH
    Upon the heath.

THIRD WITCH
    There to meet with Macbeth.

FIRST WITCH
    I come, Graymalkin!

SECOND WITCH
    Paddock calls.   10

THIRD WITCH
    Anon!

All
    Fair is foul, and foul is fair;
    Hover through the fog and filthy air.

                                        Exeunt

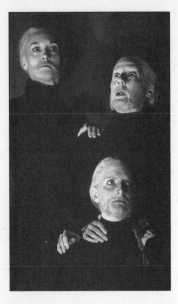

Janet Whiteside as Witch 1, Susannah Elliott-Knight as Witch 2, and Jan Chappell as
Witch 3 from the 1996 RSC production directed by Tim Albery

Joan McArthur as Witch 1, Kenneth Wynne as Witch 2, and Edward Atienza as Witch
3 in the 1952 RSC production directed by John Gielgud

Adisat Sementtsch, Wenka von Mikuliez-Radecki, and Nadja Reichardt as the witches in Schiller Theatre Company's 1992 production at the Mermaid Theatre in London
Photo: Donald Cooper

Dilys Laye as the First Witch, Susan Porrett as the Second Witch, and Joely Richardson as the Third Witch in the 1986 RSC production directed by Adrian Noble
Photo: Donald Cooper

0: Stage Direction: ***Alarum within:*** a trumpet call to arms played offstage (perhaps to suggest the sounds of battle near Duncan and his party)

0: Stage Direction: ***sergeant:*** he is called a captain in the First Folio

Set design titled "The Camp" from the 1937 production at the Old Vic directed by Michel Saint-Denis

Rare Books and Special Collections Library, University of Illinois at Urbana-Champaign

6: **broil:** battle

9: **choke their art:** be unable to use their skill or dexterity

9: **Macdonald:** Macdonwald in the First Folio

12: **western isles:** islands in the west of Scotland such as the Hebrides and perhaps Ireland

13: **kerns and gallowglasses:** Irish mercenaries, the former foot soldiers and the latter mounted; the reading in the First Folio is "Gallowgrosses."

14: **quarrel:** the First Folio reads "Quarry"

19: **minion:** a favorite of a prince; one especially loved

22: **unseamed:** undid the seam, ripped up; **nave to the chops:** from the navel to the jaw

24: **cousin:** a term of intimacy, friendship, or familiarity, it does not necessarily mean the sort of family relationship we now mean by it, but it was normally only used, except in jest, by an equal to an equal

Act 1, Scene 2]

Alarum within. Enter King [DUNCAN], MALCOLM, DONALBAIN,
LENNOX, with attendants, meeting a bleeding [sergeant].

DUNCAN
　What bloody man is that? He can report,
　As seemeth by his plight, of the revolt
　The newest state.

MALCOLM
　　　　　This is the sergeant
　Who like a good and hardy soldier fought
　'Gainst my captivity. Hail, brave friend!　　　　　　　5
　Say to the king the knowledge of the broil
　As thou didst leave it.

Sergeant
　　　　　Doubtful it stood;
　As two spent swimmers, that do cling together
　And choke their art. The merciless Macdonald—
　Worthy to be a rebel, for to that　　　　　　　　　10
　The multiplying villainies of nature
　Do swarm upon him—from the western isles
　Of kerns and [gallowglasses] is supplied;
　And Fortune, on his damnèd [quarrel] smiling,
　Showed like a rebel's whore. But all's too weak,　　　15
　For brave Macbeth—well he deserves that name—
　Disdaining Fortune, with his brandished steel,
　Which smoked with bloody execution,
　Like Valor's minion carved out his passage
　Till he faced the slave;　　　　　　　　　　　20
　Which ne'er shook hands, nor bade farewell to him,
　Till he unseamed him from the nave to the chops,
　And fixed his head upon our battlements.

DUNCAN
　O valiant cousin, worthy gentleman.

25: **'gins:** begins

26: **direful:** dreadful, dismal

28: **Mark:** listen, pay attention

30: **skipping:** thoughtless, flighty; **trust their heels:** i.e., flee

31: **Norweyan lord:** probably the king of Norway

32: **furbished:** polished

36: **sooth:** truth, or truthfully

37: **double cracks:** double, or extra, explosive charges

39: **Except:** unless

40: **memorize another Golgotha:** be remembered as Golgotha ("the place of the skull" in Hebrew) is remembered: as the place of Christ's crucifixion

45: **thane:** title equivalent to the son of an earl or the chief of a clan; in this play it is used to indicate nobility, but see Malcolm's proclamation at 5.7.92–94; **Ross:** Highland area west of Inverness

Sergeant
 As whence the sun 'gins his reflection,   25
 Shipwracking storms and direful thunders,
 So from that spring whence comfort seemed to come.
 Discomfort swells. Mark, King of Scotland, mark:
 No sooner justice had, with valor armed,
 Compelled these skipping kerns to trust their heels,   30
 But the Norweyan lord, surveying vantage,
 With furbished arms and new supplies of men
 Began a fresh assault.

DUNCAN
 Dismayed not this our captains, Macbeth and Banquo?

Sergeant
 Yes, as sparrows eagles, or the hare the lion.   35
 If I say sooth, I must report they were
 As cannons overchargèd with double cracks,
 So they doubly redoubled strokes upon the foe,
 Except they meant to bathe in reeking wounds,
 Or memorize another Golgotha,   40
 I cannot tell—but I am faint,
 My gashes cry for help.

DUNCAN
 So well thy words become thee as thy wounds;
 They smack of honor both. Go get him surgeons.
              [Exit sergeant]
 Who comes here?
        Enter ROSS and ANGUS

MALCOLM
      The worthy thane of Ross.   45

LENNOX
 What a haste looks through his eyes!
 So should he look that seems to speak things strange.

ROSS
 God save the king!

49: Fife: Macduff's home province, it lies on a peninsula between the Forth and Tay estuaries in southeastern Scotland and is therefore more susceptible to Norwegian invasion

50: Norweyan: Norwegian, spelled thus in the First Folio

52: Norway himself: the king of Norway (see line 31)

54: Cawdor: located on the Moray Firth in the Highlands and centered on the town of Inverness, this too would have been very open to Norwegian invasion

55: Bellona's: belonging to Bellona, the Roman goddess of war; **lapped:** wrapped in; **proof:** proved or tested power, originally applied to armor

58: lavish: wild or uncontrolled

60–61: Sweno, the Norways' king: The king of Norway during most of the time the events of the play take place was Magnus I the Good (1035–47) followed by Harald III (1047–66), the latter killed at the Battle of Stamford Bridge during his attempt to conquer England. The eighteenth-century editor George Steevens conjectured that "Sweno" was a marginal note that had falsely been inserted in the text and that the lines should read: "That now the Norways' king craves composition" as a single line.

61: composition: settling of debt or liability by mutual agreement

63: Saint Colme's Inch: St. Columba's Island, now called "Inchcolm" ("inch" is Scots for "island"); Colme is pronounced with two syllables

64: dollars: English name for the German *thaler*, a large silver coin, and also of coins of northern countries such as the *rigsdaler* of Denmark and the *riksdaler* of Sweden

66: bosom interest: dearest concern

DUNCAN

Whence cam'st thou, worthy thane?

ROSS

From Fife, great king,
Where the Norweyan banners flout the sky   50
And fan our people cold.
Norway himself, with terrible numbers,
Assisted by that most disloyal traitor
The thane of Cawdor, began a dismal conflict;
Till that Bellona's bridegroom, lapped in proof,   55
Confronted him with self-comparisons,
Point against point rebellious, arm 'gainst arm.
Curbing his lavish spirit; and to conclude,
The victory fell on us.

DUNCAN

Great happiness!

ROSS

That now Sweno,   60
The Norways' king, craves composition.
Nor would we deign him burial of his men
Till he disbursèd at Saint Colme's Inch
Ten thousand dollars to our general use.

DUNCAN

No more that thane of Cawdor shall deceive   65
Our bosom interest. Go, pronounce his present death,
And with his former title greet Macbeth.

ROSS

I'll see it done.

DUNCAN

What he hath lost, noble Macbeth hath won.

Exeunt

0: **Location:** usually described as being set on a heath (see 1.1.7)

0: **Scene:** After 1660, the stage has usually been set to suggest a heath with varying degrees of ruggedness, sometimes using a cave or grotto. Bogdanov's film (1997) sets this scene, and 1.1, in a garbage dump inside a disused quarry.

The witches being confronted by Macbeth, drawn by John Martin and engraved by Thomas Lupton

Mary Evans Picture Library

6: **Aroint:** begone; **rump-fed:** fed on rump meat and also with a fat rump; i.e., pampered; **runnion:** abusive term for a woman

7: **Aleppo:** inland Syrian trading city; **Tiger:** the name of the ship of which the husband is master

8: **sieve:** witches were thought to use sieves for crossing water

9: **rat without a tail:** some believed that witches often changed themselves into rats without tails, since that does not correspond to any body part

15: **ports:** perhaps seaport, with the added meaning of opening or gate

16: **quarters:** the four winds

17: **shipman's card:** a mariner's compass and/or navigation chart

Act 1, Scene 3]

FIRST WITCH
Where hast thou been, sister?

SECOND WITCH
Killing swine.

THIRD WITCH
Sister, where thou?

FIRST WITCH
A sailor's wife had chestnuts in her lap,
And munched, and munched, and munched. "Give me," quoth I.   5
"Aroint thee, witch!" the rump-fed runnion cries.
Her husband's to Aleppo gone, master o' th' Tiger,
But in a sieve I'll thither sail,
And, like a rat without a tail,
I'll do, I'll do, and I'll do.   10

SECOND WITCH
I'll give thee a wind.

FIRST WITCH
Th' art kind.

THIRD WITCH
And I another.

FIRST WITCH
I myself have all the other,
And the very ports they blow,   15
All the quarters that they know
I' th' shipman's card.
I will drain him dry as hay.

20: **penthouse lid:** eyelid

21: **forbid:** accursed

22: **nine times nine:** nine, being three times three, is a mystical number; Scottish folklore also held nine times nine as a charm with magical powers

23: **peak:** waste away

24: **bark:** vessel; **lost:** destroyed

28: **pilot:** helmsman; **thumb:** the loss of the pilot's thumb, and perhaps his hand, may explain the difficulty with his vessel in the next line

29: **Wracked:** wrecked, but also tormented

32: **weird:** destined or having the power to control fate or destiny; the "weird sisters" also refers to the Fates, of which there were three; the First Folio reads "weyward," an obsolete form of "weird"

tracks 5-7

38–88:
Orson Welles as Macbeth and Robert Warrick as Banquo
Stephen Dillane as Macbeth and Adam Kotz as Banquo

33: **Posters of:** messengers ("of" is used in the sense of "over" or "to")

39: **How far is't called:** how far do people say it is; **Forres:** the First Folio reads "Soris" but editors since 1725 have emended this to Forres, a town east of Inverness, which is near the site of the battles described in the previous scene

39–40: "What are these / So withered and so wild in their attire":
Janet Whiteside as Witch 1, Susannah Elliott-Knight as Witch 2, Jan Chappell as Witch 3, Roger Allam as Macbeth, and Philip Quast as Banquo in the 1996 RSC production directed by Tim Albery

Photo: Donald Cooper

Sleep shall neither night nor day
Hang upon his penthouse lid.   20
He shall live a man forbid.
Weary sev'nnights, nine times nine,
Shall he dwindle, peak and pine.
Though his bark cannot be lost,
Yet it shall be tempest-tossed.   25
Look what I have.

SECOND WITCH
Show me, show me.

FIRST WITCH
Here I have a pilot's thumb,
Wracked as homeward he did come.   *Drum within*

THIRD WITCH
A drum, a drum!   30
Macbeth doth come.

All
The weird sisters, hand in hand,
Posters of the sea and land,
Thus do go about, about,
Thrice to thine and thrice to mine   35
And thrice again, to make up nine.
Peace! the charm's wound up.

Enter MACBETH and BANQUO

MACBETH
So foul and fair a day I have not seen.

BANQUO
How far is't called to [Forres]? What are these
So withered and so wild in their attire,   40
That look not like the inhabitants o' th' earth,
And yet are on't? Live you, or are you aught
That man may question? You seem to understand me,
By each at once her choppy finger laying

38–88:
Orson Welles as Macbeth and Robert Warrick as Banquo
Stephen Dillane as Macbeth and Adam Kotz as Banquo

45: **should be:** look as though you are

46: **beards:** facial hair was associated with witchcraft

48: **Glamis:** the area north of Dundee on the Firth of Tay; Shakespeare probably pronounced the word with two syllables though we pronounce it with one

50: Scene: there is a tradition, going back as far as Kemble (1788), of the witches kneeling at this point

53: **fantastical:** imaginary or a hallucination

55: **present grace:** his current noble title as Thane of Glamis

56: **of noble having and of royal hope:** i.e., the promised title of Thane of Cawdor and of the prediction he will be king at a later time

57: **rapt withal:** entranced or enraptured with it

58: **seeds of time:** sources of the future, with a play on the word "grain" in the next line

Upon her skinny lips. You should be women,   45
And yet your beards forbid me to interpret
That you are so.

MACBETH

               Speak, if you can. What are you?

FIRST WITCH
  All hail, Macbeth! Hail to thee, thane of Glamis!

SECOND WITCH
  All hail, Macbeth! Hail to thee, thane of Cawdor!

THIRD WITCH
  All hail, Macbeth! Thou shalt be king hereafter!   50

BANQUO
  Good sir, why do you start; and seem to fear
  Things that do sound so fair? —I' th' name of truth,
  Are ye fantastical, or that indeed
  Which outwardly ye show? My noble partner
  You greet with present grace and great prediction   55
  Of noble having and of royal hope,
  That he seems rapt withal. To me you speak not.
  If you can look into the seeds of time,
  And say which grain will grow and which will not,
  Speak then to me, who neither beg nor fear   60
  Your favors nor your hate.

FIRST WITCH
  Hail!

SECOND WITCH
  Hail!

THIRD WITCH
  Hail!

FIRST WITCH
  Lesser than Macbeth, and greater.   65

tracks 5-7

38–88:
Orson Welles as Macbeth and Robert Warrick as Banquo
Stephen Dillane as Macbeth and Adam Kotz as Banquo

70: **imperfect:** incomplete

71: **Sinel:** Macbeth's father, but this spelling comes from an error in Shakespeare's sources and Macbeth's father's name was really spelt "Finele"

72–73: **The thane of Cawdor lives, / A prosperous gentleman:** This contradicts lines 1.1.55–1.1.59. According to those lines, Bellona's bridegroom, Macbeth, knows that although the thane of Cawdor may still be alive, he is hardly a prosperous gentleman and may in fact be a rebel. This contradiction may be the result of an imperfect revision of the manuscript used to print the First Folio.

78: Stage Direction: ***WITCHES vanish:*** In the post-1660 theatre, they regularly flew away, as was the case with Davenant's production in 1673. At the Globe, they could not have been flown since there is no evidence of machinery capable of flying more than one actor; this was true of Blackfriars also. It is possible that they descended through the stage trap. In the 1740s, Garrick had the witches sink. Stage hangings (curtains and the like) and stage smoke have been used to cover their exit.

84: **insane root:** plant that produces insanity or hallucinations, perhaps hemlock, henbane, or deadly nightshade

SECOND WITCH
Not so happy, yet much happier.

THIRD WITCH
Thou shalt get kings, though thou be none.
So all hail, Macbeth and Banquo!

FIRST WITCH
Banquo and Macbeth, all hail!

MACBETH
Stay, you imperfect speakers, tell me more.   70
By Sinel's death I know I am thane of Glamis;
But how of Cawdor? The thane of Cawdor lives,
A prosperous gentleman; and to be king
Stands not within the prospect of belief,
No more than to be Cawdor. Say from whence   75
You owe this strange intelligence? Or why
Upon this blasted heath you stop our way
With such prophetic greeting? Speak, I charge you.

WITCHES vanish

BANQUO
The earth hath bubbles, as the water has,
And these are of them. Whither are they vanished?   80

MACBETH
Into the air; and what seemed corporal melted
As breath into the wind. Would they had stayed!

BANQUO
Were such things here as we do speak about?
Or have we eaten on the insane root
That takes the reason prisoner?   85

MACBETH
Your children shall be kings.

BANQUO
                    You shall be king.

tracks 5-7

38–88:
Orson Welles as Macbeth and Robert Warrick as Banquo
Stephen Dillane as Macbeth and Adam Kotz as Banquo

93: **Silenced with that:** speechless with wonder

97: **hail:** the First Folio reads "Tale," though most editors since 1709 have emended this to "hail" as is done here; "as thick as hail" describes the number and rapidity of the messengers' or posts' arrivals

98: **Came:** "Can" in the First Folio

100–103: **We are sent...pay thee:** their visit and the thanks they bring from Duncan are not payment for services but a means to have Macbeth come to Duncan

104: **earnest:** a small payment to seal a bargain with a promise of greater reward later

106: **addition:** increase in his titles

107–109: Scene: The reactions of Macbeth and Banquo to this sudden fulfillment of half of the witches' prophesy has been variously staged. In the nineteenth century, both Charles Kean and Henry Irving are reported to have reacted violently, the former clenching and unclenching his right fist rapidly. Banquo's "What, can the devil speak true?" is frequently said as an aside to Macbeth (as in the 1999 RSC production, when Banquo spoke into Macbeth's ear) or to the audience (as John Woodvine did at the RSC in 1976). Often Ross and/or Angus present Macbeth with a document, medal, or chain of office for his new position as Thane of Cawdor.

109: **borrowed:** usurped

MACBETH
    And thane of Cawdor too. Went it not so?

BANQUO
    To the selfsame tune and words. Who's here?

Enter ROSS and ANGUS

ROSS
    The king hath happily received, Macbeth,
    The news of thy success; and when he reads   90
    Thy personal venture in the rebels' fight,
    His wonders and his praises do contend
    Which should be thine or his. Silenced with that,
    In viewing o'er the rest o' th' selfsame day,
    He finds thee in the stout Norweyan ranks,   95
    Nothing afeard of what thyself didst make,
    Strange images of death. As thick as [hail]
    [Came] post with post; and every one did bear
    Thy praises in his kingdom's great defence,
    And poured them down before him.

ANGUS
                            We are sent   100
    To give thee from our royal master thanks,
    Only to herald thee into his sight,
    Not pay thee.

ROSS
    And, for an earnest of a greater honor,
    He bade me, from him, call thee thane of Cawdor.   105
    In which addition, hail, most worthy thane!
    For it is thine.

BANQUO
                            What, can the devil speak true?

MACBETH
    The thane of Cawdor lives. Why do you dress me
    In borrowed robes?

111: was combined: conspired

112: line: assist or reinforce

113: vantage: advantage

117: the greatest is behind: the greatest (the kingship) is still to happen

120: home: fully or completely

121: enkindle: incite

122: "But 'tis strange": Martin Shaw as Banquo in *The Tragedy of Macbeth* (1971) directed by Roman Polanski

Courtesy: Douglas Lanier

126: deepest consequence: greatest importance, in contrast to "trifles" in previous line

132: earnest: partial payment as promise of a future larger transaction

135: unfix my hair: cause my hair to stand on end

ANGUS

     Who was the thane lives yet;
But under heavy judgment bears that life   110
Which he deserves to lose. Whether he was combined
With those of Norway, or did line the rebel
With hidden help and vantage, or that with both
He labored in his country's wreck, I know not;
But treasons capital, confessed and proved,   115
Have overthrown him.

MACBETH

    [*Aside*] Glamis, and thane of Cawdor!
The greatest is behind.
    [*To Ross and Angus*] Thanks for your pains.
[*To Banquo*] Do you not hope your children shall be kings,
When those that gave the thane of Cawdor to me
Promised no less to them?

BANQUO

    [*To Macbeth*] That trusted home   120
Might yet enkindle you unto the crown,
Besides the thane of Cawdor. But 'tis strange.
And oftentimes, to win us to our harm,
The instruments of darkness tell us truths,
Win us with honest trifles, to betray's   125
In deepest consequence.—
Cousins, a word, I pray you.

MACBETH

    [*Aside*] Two truths are told,
As happy prologues to the swelling act
Of the imperial theme.—I thank you, gentlemen.
[*Aside*] This supernatural soliciting   130
Cannot be ill, cannot be good. If ill,
Why hath it given me earnest of success,
Commencing in a truth? I am thane of Cawdor.
If good, why do I yield to that suggestion
Whose horrid image doth unfix my hair   135
And make my seated heart knock at my ribs,

137: Against the use of nature: in an unnatural way; **Present fears:** current fears

139: fantastical: imaginary

140: single state of man: ordinary or normal human condition; **function:** the power to act

142: rapt: enraptured

145–46: strange garments, cleave not to their mold / But with the aid of use: new clothes do not fit properly until they have been regularly worn

147: Time and the hour runs through the roughest day: even a difficult day comes to an end

149: wrought: agitated

150: things forgotten: memories

154: interim having weighed it: having thought about it in the interim

155: our free hearts: openly, candidly

Against the use of nature? Present fears
Are less than horrible imaginings.
My thought, whose murder yet is but fantastical,
Shakes so my single state of man that function   140
Is smothered in surmise, and nothing is
But what is not.

BANQUO
                        Look, how our partner's rapt.

MACBETH
[*Still aside*] If chance will have me king, why, chance may crown me,
Without my stir.

BANQUO
                        New honors come upon him,
Like our strange garments, cleave not to their mold   145
But with the aid of use.

MACBETH
                        [*Still aside*] Come what come may,
Time and the hour runs through the roughest day.

BANQUO
Worthy Macbeth, we stay upon your leisure.

MACBETH
Give me your favor. My dull brain was wrought
With things forgotten. Kind gentlemen, your pains   150
Are registered where every day I turn
The leaf to read them. Let us toward the king.
[*Aside to Banquo*] Think upon what hath chanced, and at more time,
The interim having weighed it, let us speak
Our free hearts each to other.

BANQUO
                        Very gladly.   155

MACBETH
Till then, enough. Come, friends.
                                            Exeunt

0: Location: some describe this scene as set in Duncan's camp and others as set in a room in the castle at Forres

0: Stage Direction: *Flourish*: a trumpet fanfare

10: **studied:** well-versed, practiced

16–17: **The sin...on me:** I was worried I would not appear properly grateful

17: **before:** ahead, in deserving

20: **proportion:** correct apportionment

Act 1, Scene 4]

Flourish. Enter DUNCAN, MALCOLM, DONALBAIN,
LENNOX, and attendants.

DUNCAN
Is execution done on Cawdor?
Or [are] not those in commission yet returned?

MALCOLM
My liege, they are not yet come back.
But I have spoke with one that saw him die,
Who did report that very frankly he   5
Confessed his treasons, implored your highness' pardon
And set forth a deep repentance.
Nothing in his life became him
Like the leaving it. He died
As one that had been studied in his death   10
To throw away the dearest thing he owed,
As 'twere a careless trifle.

DUNCAN
                    There's no art
To find the mind's construction in the face.
He was a gentleman on whom I built
An absolute trust.
                    Enter MACBETH, BANQUO, ROSS, and ANGUS
                    O worthiest cousin!   15
The sin of my ingratitude even now
Was heavy on me. Thou art so far before
That swiftest wing of recompense is slow
To overtake thee. Would thou hadst less deserved,
That the proportion both of thanks and payment   20
Might have been mine. Only I have left to say,
More is thy due than more than all can pay.

25–26: our duties...and servants: we are to your rule as children and servants are to their father and master

29: plant: establish

30–33: "Noble Banquo...my heart": Nicolas Selby as Duncan, Martin Shaw as Banquo, and Jon Finch as Macbeth in *The Tragedy of Macbeth* (1971) directed by Roman Polanski
Courtesy: Douglas Lanier

35: Wanton: unrestrained

40: Prince of Cumberland: similar to the Prince of Wales in England, the heir to the throne

40: Scene: In almost all productions, the naming of Malcolm as Duncan's successor produces a reaction from Macbeth. Sometimes Banquo also reacts.

41–43: Not unaccompanied...deservers: not only will Malcolm be honored but also all the others, such as Macbeth and Banquo, who have earned honor

43: Inverness: Macbeth's castle, not his seat at Glamis, which is further south

46: harbinger: one sent ahead to provide lodgings for an army or a royal party

MACBETH
>The service and the loyalty I owe,
>In doing it, pays itself. Your highness' part
>Is to receive our duties; and our duties   25
>Are to your throne and state children and servants,
>Which do but what they should by doing every thing
>Safe toward your love and honor.

DUNCAN
>   Welcome hither.
>I have begun to plant thee and will labor
>To make thee full of growing. Noble Banquo,   30
>That hast no less deserved, nor must be known
>No less to have done so, let me enfold thee
>And hold thee to my heart.

BANQUO
>   There if I grow,
>The harvest is your own.

DUNCAN
>   My plenteous joys,
>Wanton in fulness, seek to hide themselves   35
>In drops of sorrow. Sons, kinsmen, thanes,
>And you whose places are the nearest, know
>We will establish our estate upon
>Our eldest, Malcolm, whom we name hereafter
>The Prince of Cumberland; which honor must   40
>Not unaccompanied invest him only,
>But signs of nobleness, like stars, shall shine
>On all deservers. From hence to Inverness,
>And bind us further to you.

MACBETH
>The rest is labor which is not used for you.   45
>I'll be myself the harbinger and make joyful
>The hearing of my wife with your approach;
>So humbly take my leave.

49–54: Scene: This aside by Macbeth is uttered as he exits and, typically, is delivered more directly to the audience than some of the other asides.

49–50: step / On which I must fall down: i.e., the prince is an obstacle to Macbeth becoming king

50: or else o'erleap: to leap over Malcolm will require the killing of Duncan and probably also of Malcolm

51: in my way it lies: i.e., if Malcolm becomes king, Macbeth cannot become king in a natural manner of succession

53: The eye wink at the hand: let my eye ignore what my hand does

55: True, worthy Banquo: Duncan may be responding to what Banquo has said about Macbeth during Macbeth's aside.

DUNCAN

My worthy Cawdor.

MACBETH

[*Aside*] The Prince of Cumberland! That is a step
On which I must fall down, or else o'erleap,   50
For in my way it lies. Stars, hide your fires;
Let not light see my black and deep desires.
The eye wink at the hand; yet let that be,
Which the eye fears, when it is done, to see.

Exit

DUNCAN

True, worthy Banquo. He is full so valiant,   55
And in his commendations I am fed;
It is a banquet to me. Let's after him,
Whose care is gone before to bid us welcome.
It is a peerless kinsman.

Flourish. Exeunt.

0: Location: traditionally described as being set inside Macbeth's castle at Inverness

0: Stage Direction: The First Folio reads, "*Enter Macbeths Wife alone with a Letter.*" The stage direction has been emended to describe the action taking place.

1–11: Scene: We assume from the stage direction that she is alone means that her reading of the letter ought to be very private. Some actresses have paced, some have been seated, and others, such as Dench (RSC 1976), seem to have already committed the contents of the letter to memory. Polanski, who moved the first half of this scene to before 1.4, has Lady Macbeth (Francesca Annis) receive the letter from a mounted messenger and read it silently in the courtyard of the castle and only say lines 8–11 aloud to us. She then folds the letter and while she delivers the remainder of her speech in a voice-over, she goes to her chamber and locks the letter in a chest.

tracks 8-9

1–27:
Sybil Thorndike as Lady Macbeth

2: **perfect'st report:** reliable evidence

5: **missives:** writings carried by messengers

15: **nearest way:** most direct course

17: **illness:** wickedness

17–18: **What thou wouldst highly, / That wouldst thou holily:** i.e., what you value highly you wish to get by moral or holy means

23: **pour my spirits in thine ear:** i.e., transfer my power or energy to you

25: **golden round:** crown

26: **metaphysical:** supernatural or only imaginary

Act 1, Scene 5]

Enter [LADY MACBETH], alone [reading] a letter

LADY MACBETH

They met me in the day of success, and I have learned by the
perfect'st report, they have more in them than mortal knowledge.
When I burned in desire to question them further, they made
themselves air, into which they vanished. Whiles I stood rapt in
the wonder of it, came missives from the king, who all-hailed me   5
"Thane of Cawdor"; by which title, before, these weird sisters
saluted me, and referred me to the coming on of time, with
"Hail, king that shalt be!" This have I thought good to deliver
thee, my dearest partner of greatness, that thou mightst not lose
the dues of rejoicing, by being ignorant of what greatness is   10
promised thee. Lay it to thy heart, and farewell.
Glamis thou art, and Cawdor; and shalt be
What thou art promised. Yet do I fear thy nature;
It is too full o' th' milk of human kindness
To catch the nearest way. Thou wouldst be great,   15
Art not without ambition, but without
The illness should attend it. What thou wouldst highly,
That wouldst thou holily; wouldst not play false,
And yet wouldst wrongly win. Thou'd'st have, great Glamis,
That which cries "Thus thou must do," if thou have it;   20
And that which rather thou dost fear to do
Than wishest should be undone. Hie thee hither,
That I may pour my spirits in thine ear;
And chastise with the valor of my tongue
All that impedes thee from the golden round,   25
Which fate and metaphysical aid doth seem
To have thee crowned withal.

Enter a messenger

What is your tidings?

Messenger
The king comes here tonight.

28: Scene: ***Thou'rt mad to say it!:*** This almost always produces a reaction of shock and amazement from the actress playing Lady Macbeth. However, some directors, Polanski for instance, cut the messenger and this short speech and run Lady Macbeth's two long speeches into one.

28: **mad:** insane, but almost in a joking, disbelieving sense

tracks 10-12

35–70:
Harriet Walter as Lady Macbeth and Hugh Ross as Macbeth
Pamela Brown as Lady Macbeth and Alec Guinness as Macbeth

35: **raven:** the raven was thought to be ominous
36: **fatal:** directed by fate, or the Fates, as well as an entrance that will be fatal to Duncan
38: **unsex me:** i.e., strip from me the soft and gentle qualities of womanhood
40: **direst:** most dreadful
41: **remorse:** pity
42: **compunctious visitings:** remorseful feelings; **nature:** natural feelings
43: **fell:** deadly, fierce
43–44: **keep peace...effect and it:** prevent my purpose, the murder of Duncan, from being achieved
44: **it:** "hit" in the First Folio
45: **take my milk for gall:** change my breast milk to gall (bile)
46: **sightless:** invisible
47: **wait on nature's mischief:** wait as attendants on the evil of Nature
48: **pall:** cover with a pall, as in a pall of smoke; a pall is also the cloth used to cover a coffin at a funeral; **dunnest:** darkest
49: **keen:** sharp
54: **ignorant present:** awareness of the present moment only

LADY MACBETH
                    Thou'rt mad to say it!
Is not thy master with him, who, were't so,
Would have informed for preparation?   30

Messenger
    So please you, it is true. Our thane is coming.
    One of my fellows had the speed of him,
    Who, almost dead for breath, had scarcely more
    Than would make up his message.

LADY MACBETH
                    Give him tending;
    He brings great news.

                                                    Exit messenger
                        The raven himself is hoarse   35
That croaks the fatal entrance of Duncan
Under my battlements. Come you spirits
That tend on mortal thoughts, unsex me here,
And fill me from the crown to the toe top-full
Of direst cruelty. Make thick my blood.   40
Stop up th' access and passage to remorse,
That no compunctious visitings of nature
Shake my fell purpose, nor keep peace between
Th' effect and [it]. Come to my woman's breasts,
And take my milk for gall, you murd'ring ministers,   45
Wherever in your sightless substances
You wait on nature's mischief. Come, thick night,
And pall thee in the dunnest smoke of hell,
That my keen knife see not the wound it makes,
Nor heaven peep through the blanket of the dark   50
To cry "Hold, hold."

                                                    Enter MACBETH
                        Great Glamis, worthy Cawdor,
Greater than both, by the all-hail hereafter.
Thy letters have transported me beyond
This ignorant present, and I feel now
The future in the instant.

35–70:
Harriet Walter as Lady Macbeth and Hugh Ross as Macbeth
Pamela Brown as Lady Macbeth and Alec Guinness as Macbeth

60: **beguile the time:** to deceive those around you

61: **Look like the time:** conform to present practices

65: **dispatch:** management, with a secondary meaning of killing

67: **solely sovereign:** absolute; **sway:** power

68–70: "Only look up clear; / To alter favor ever is to fear. / Leave all the rest to me": Laila Robins as Lady Macbeth and Robert Cuccioli as Macbeth in The Shakespeare Theatre of New Jersey's 2004 production directed by Bonnie J. Monte
Photo: Gerry Goodstein

68: **look up clear:** appear to be happy

69: **favor:** appearance or expression; **fear:** to create or have fear

MACBETH
       My dearest love,   55
  Duncan comes here tonight.

LADY MACBETH
        And when goes hence?

MACBETH
  Tomorrow, as he purposes.

LADY MACBETH
        O, never
  Shall sun that morrow see.
  Your face, my thane, is as a book where men
  May read strange matters. To beguile the time,   60
  Look like the time. Bear welcome in your eye,
  Your hand, your tongue. Look like the innocent flower,
  But be the serpent under't. He that's coming
  Must be provided for; and you shall put
  This night's great business into my dispatch,   65
  Which shall to all our nights and days to come
  Give solely sovereign sway and masterdom.

MACBETH
  We will speak further.

LADY MACBETH
        Only look up clear;
  To alter favor ever is to fear.
  Leave all the rest to me.   70
               Exeunt

0: Location: before Macbeth's castle at Inverness

0: Stage Direction: **hautboys:** ancestors of the oboe but much more powerful and used for outdoor ceremonials; **torches:** the inclusion of torches in the stage direction in the First Folio must indicate that the scene is to be imagined as happening at night

1: **seat:** location

4: **temple-haunting martlet:** house martin, a type of bird noted for nesting around churches; the First Folio reads "Bartlet"

5: **mansionry:** nest building

6: **wooingly:** enticingly or invitingly; **jutty:** projection

7: **coign of vantage:** projecting corner of building that provides a good view

8. **pendent bed and procreant cradle:** suspended nest for breeding

12–13: **The love...thank as love:** the love of our subjects is sometimes inconvenient but we are still grateful for it

14: **God 'ild:** God yield, meaning "thank you"

15: **thank us for your trouble:** your troubles are due to your love for us

17: **single business:** simple effort

20: **late dignities:** recent honors

21: **hermits:** beadsmen, those endowed to pray for others; in England and Scotland often a semi-official or licensed position

Act 1, Scene 6]

Hautboys and torches. Enter DUNCAN, MALCOLM,
DONALBAIN, BANQUO, LENNOX, MACDUFF,
ROSS, ANGUS, and attendants.

DUNCAN
This castle hath a pleasant seat. The air
Nimbly and sweetly recommends itself
Unto our gentle senses.

BANQUO
                        This guest of summer,
The temple-haunting [martlet], does approve,
By his loved mansionry, that the heaven's breath   5
Smells wooingly here. No jutty, frieze,
Buttress, nor coign of vantage, but this bird
Hath made his pendent bed and procreant cradle.
Where they most breed and haunt, I have observed,
The air is delicate.   10
                                Enter LADY MACBETH

DUNCAN
See, see, our honored hostess!
The love that follows us sometime is our trouble,
Which still we thank as love. Herein I teach you
How you shall bid God 'ild us for your pains,
And thank us for your trouble.

LADY MACBETH
                        All our service   15
In every point twice done and then done double
Were poor and single business to contend
Against those honors deep and broad wherewith
Your majesty loads our house. For those of old,
And the late dignities heaped up to them,   20
We rest your hermits.

22: **coursed:** pursued

23: **purveyor:** servant who makes the preparations for the arrival of his master

24: **holp:** archaic form of helped

27: **Have theirs:** have their own servants; **theirs, in compt:** what is ours, held in trust or on account, from the king. "Compt" is an obsolete form of count or account; hence, the audit of this account referred to in the next line.

29: **Still:** always

Edna Thomas as Lady Macbeth in the 1936 production at the New Lafayette Theatre directed by Orson Welles
Library of Congress, Music Division, Federal Theatre Project Collection

DUNCAN

Where's the thane of Cawdor?
We coursed him at the heels, and had a purpose
To be his purveyor, but he rides well;
And his great love, sharp as his spur, hath holp him
To his home before us. Fair and noble hostess,   25
We are your guest tonight.

LADY MACBETH

Your servants ever
Have theirs, themselves, and what is theirs, in compt,
To make their audit at your highness' pleasure,
Still to return your own.

DUNCAN

Give me your hand;
Conduct me to mine host. We love him highly,   30
And shall continue our graces towards him.
By your leave, hostess.

Exeunt

0: Stage Direction: ***torches***: though the scene is clearly set indoors, torches are needed since it is night; ***Sewer***: chief waiter or butler; ***service***: tableware (knives, cups, and the like); ***over the stage***: across the stage

1–28:
Simon Russell Beale as Macbeth
Orson Welles as Macbeth

tracks 13–15

1–2: **If it were...quickly:** if the murder of Duncan will end the matter, then it would be best to get it over with
2: **assassination:** this is the first use of the word, as a noun, in English
3: **trammel up:** entrap the consequences, as in a net
4: **his surcease success:** Duncan's death successfully accomplished; "success" also puns on the royal succession that Macbeth hopes will be his
5: **be-all and the end-all:** this Shakespearean coinage is still in popular use
6: **bank and shoal:** sandbank and shallows; "shoal" is "Schoole" in the First Folio
7: **jump the life to come:** risk one's immortal soul
17: **faculties:** power or authority; **meek:** humbly, gently
18: **clear:** honesty or innocent
19: **plead:** as in a court of law; **trumpet-tongued:** blaringly, as with the voice of a trumpet
20: **taking-off:** murder
22: **Striding the blast:** walking or striding upon the gale (blast = wind); **cherubin:** although cherubin are popularly depicted as winged infant angels, Shakespeare seems to have in mind the more technical definition: the second order of a rather more powerful angel, horsed on (riding) the winds
23: **sightless couriers of the air:** the winds
28: **on the other:** on the other side of the mount

28–80:
Pamela Brown as Lady Macbeth and Alec Guinness as Macbeth
Fay Bainter as Lady Macbeth and Orson Welles as Macbeth

tracks 16–18

Hautboys and torches. Enter a Sewer and divers
servants with dishes and service over the stage.
Then enter MACBETH.

MACBETH
If it were done when 'tis done, then 'twere well
It were done quickly. If the assassination
Could trammel up the consequence, and catch
With his surcease success, that but this blow
Might be the be-all and the end-all here,   5
But here, upon this bank and [shoal] of time,
We'd jump the life to come. But in these cases
We still have judgment here, that we but teach
Bloody instructions, which, being taught, return
To plague th' inventor. This evenhanded justice   10
Commends the ingredients of our poisoned chalice
To our own lips. He's here in double trust:
First, as I am his kinsman and his subject,
Strong both against the deed; then, as his host,
Who should against his murderer shut the door,   15
Not bear the knife myself. Besides, this Duncan
Hath borne his faculties so meek, hath been
So clear in his great office, that his virtues
Will plead like angels, trumpet-tongued, against
The deep damnation of his taking-off;   20
And pity, like a naked newborn babe,
Striding the blast, or heaven's cherubin, horsed
Upon the sightless couriers of the air,
Shall blow the horrid deed in every eye,
That tears shall drown the wind. I have no spur   25
To prick the sides of my intent, but only
Vaulting ambition, which o'erleaps itself
And falls on the other.

Enter LADY [MACBETH]

How now? What news?

28–80:
Pamela Brown as Lady Macbeth and Alec Guinness as Macbeth
Fay Bainter as Lady Macbeth and Orson Welles as Macbeth

29: **supped:** finished dining

33: **Golden:** excellent

34: **newest gloss:** new and shiny

37: **green and pale:** hungover

45: **cat i' th' adage:** the adage of the cat who wanted to eat fish but did not want to get its feet wet

47: **do:** the First Folio reads "no"

48: **break:** broach, propose

49: **durst:** dared

49–51: "When you durst do it, then you were a man; / And to be more than what you were, you would / Be so much more the man": Colleen Dewhurst as Lady Macbeth and Roy Poole as Macbeth in the Public Theater's 1957 production directed by Stuart Vaughan
Photo: George E. Joseph

LADY MACBETH
    He has almost supped. Why have you left the chamber?

MACBETH
    Hath he asked for me?

LADY MACBETH
                  Know you not he has?   30

MACBETH
    We will proceed no further in this business.
    He hath honored me of late; and I have bought
    Golden opinions from all sorts of people,
    Which would be worn now in their newest gloss,
    Not cast aside so soon.

LADY MACBETH
                  Was the hope drunk   35
    Wherein you dressed yourself? Hath it slept since?
    And wakes it now, to look so green and pale
    At what it did so freely? From this time
    Such I account thy love. Art thou afeard
    To be the same in thine own act and valor   40
    As thou art in desire? Wouldst thou have that
    Which thou esteem'st the ornament of life,
    And live a coward in thine own esteem,
    Letting "I dare not" wait upon "I would,"
    Like the poor cat i' th' adage?

MACBETH
                  Prithee, peace!   45
    I dare do all that may become a man.
    Who dares [do] more is none.

LADY MACBETH
                  What beast was't, then,
    That made you break this enterprise to me?
    When you durst do it, then you were a man;
    And, to be more than what you were, you would   50

tracks 16-18

28–80:
Pamela Brown as Lady Macbeth and Alec Guinness as Macbeth
Fay Bainter as Lady Macbeth and Orson Welles as Macbeth

51: **Nor:** neither

52: **adhere:** apply; **make both:** make both apply to the proposed killing of Duncan

53: **They have made themselves:** time and place have now made themselves available; **their fitness:** their very convenience

54: **unmake:** unnerve

60: **sticking place:** notch on a crossbow or stringed instrument that holds the string taut

63: **chamberlains:** servants of the bed chamber

64: **wassail:** both liquor and carousing with the same

65: **warder:** guard

66: **fume:** mist, delusion

67: **limbeck:** alembic, that part of a distilling device where the fumes gather; **swinish:** gross, beastly

68: **drenchèd natures:** soaked mental faculties and therefore, useless

70: **put upon:** blame

71: **spongy:** soaked with liquor, as a sponge

72: **quell:** killing

73: **undaunted:** fearless; **mettle:** spirit and/or valor

74: **received:** accepted

Be so much more the man. Nor time nor place
Did then adhere, and yet you would make both.
They have made themselves, and that their fitness now
Does unmake you. I have given suck, and know
How tender 'tis to love the babe that milks me.   55
I would, while it was smiling in my face,
Have plucked my nipple from his boneless gums,
And dashed the brains out, had I so sworn as you
Have done to this.

MACBETH
          If we should fail?

LADY MACBETH
            We fail!
But screw your courage to the sticking place,   60
And we'll not fail. When Duncan is asleep,
Whereto the rather shall his day's hard journey
Soundly invite him, his two chamberlains
Will I with wine and wassail so convince
That memory, the warder of the brain,   65
Shall be a fume, and the receipt of reason
A limbeck only. When in swinish sleep
Their drenchèd natures lie as in a death,
What cannot you and I perform upon
The unguarded Duncan? What not put upon   70
His spongy officers, who shall bear the guilt
Of our great quell?

MACBETH
          Bring forth men-children only,
For thy undaunted mettle should compose
Nothing but males. Will it not be received,
When we have marked with blood those sleepy two   75
Of his own chamber and used their very daggers,
That they have done't?

28–80:
Pamela Brown as Lady Macbeth and Alec Guinness as Macbeth
Fay Bainter as Lady Macbeth and Orson Welles as Macbeth

79–80: bend up / Each corporal agent: gather all my physical strength

81: mock: deceive

82: "False face must hide what the false heart doth know": Ian McKellen
as Macbeth and Judi Dench as Lady Macbeth in the 1976 RSC production directed
by Trevor Nunn

Photo: Donald Cooper

LADY MACBETH
                    Who dares receive it other,
        As we shall make our griefs and clamor roar
        Upon his death?

MACBETH
                    I am settled, and bend up
        Each corporal agent to this terrible feat.   80
        Away, and mock the time with fairest show.
        False face must hide what the false heart doth know.

                                        Exeunt

[Macbeth

Act 2

0: Stage Direction: *with a torch before him*: There is a certain ambiguity to this direction. Either Fleance is carrying a torch held in front of him or there is a torchbearer preceding him.

5: **husbandry:** careful housekeeping, but with a sexual double meaning

6: **that:** probably refers to Banquo's dagger

7: **heavy summons:** strong desire to sleep

10: Stage Direction: *servant with a torch*: There is a significant tradition of having this particular servant, the one constantly in attendance on Macbeth, played by the same actor who plays Seyton later in the play. This is not so much a case of doubling as it is of assigning a name to a generically named character. It takes on a good deal more significance in 3.3, where many productions (such as Polanski, Bogdanov, and Nunn [RSC 1976]) have Servant/Seyton as the Third Murderer.

14: **largess:** presents; **offices:** rooms used for household work

15: **withal:** with

16: **shut up:** summed up

Act 2, Scene 1]

Enter BANQUO and FLEANCE, with a torch before him

BANQUO
How goes the night, boy?

FLEANCE
The moon is down. I have not heard the clock.

BANQUO
And she goes down at twelve.

FLEANCE
I take't, 'tis later, sir.

BANQUO
Hold, take my sword. There's husbandry in heaven,   5
Their candles are all out. Take thee that too.
A heavy summons lies like lead upon me,
And yet I would not sleep. Merciful powers,
Restrain in me the cursèd thoughts that nature
Gives way to in repose!

Enter MACBETH and a servant with a torch

Give me my sword—Who's there?   10

MACBETH
A friend.

BANQUO
What, sir, not yet at rest? The king's abed.
He hath been in unusual pleasure, and
Sent forth great largess to your offices.
This diamond he greets your wife withal,   15
By the name of most kind hostess, and shut up
In measureless content.

17–19: Being unprepared...should free have wrought: We did the best we could on the spur of the moment but would have done better with more time to prepare (wrought = worked)

22: "I think not of them": Robert Cuccioli as Macbeth and Michael Stewart as Banquo in The Shakespeare Theatre of New Jersey's 2004 production directed by Bonnie J. Monte
Photo: Gerry Goodstein

23: entreat an hour to serve: find a convenient time

26: cleave to my consent: agree with my plans

28: still: always

29: bosom franchised: myself free from obligation

MACBETH
                    Being unprepared,
Our will became the servant to defect,
Which else should free have wrought.

BANQUO
    All's well.   20
    I dreamt last night of the three weird sisters.
    To you they have showed some truth.

MACBETH
                    I think not of them.
Yet, when we can entreat an hour to serve,
We would spend it in some words upon that business,
If you would grant the time.

BANQUO
                    At your kind'st leisure.   25

MACBETH
    If you shall cleave to my consent, when 'tis,
    It shall make honor for you.

BANQUO
                    So I lose none
In seeking to augment it, but still keep
My bosom franchised and allegiance clear,
I shall be counseled.

MACBETH
                    Good repose the while.   30

BANQUO
    Thanks, sir. The like to you.

                          Exeunt BANQUO [and FLEANCE]

MACBETH
    Go bid thy mistress, when my drink is ready,
    She strike upon the bell. Get thee to bed.

                                        Exit servant

34–50: Scene: On Shakespeare's stage, the dagger that Macbeth sees would have been entirely "a dagger of the mind." However, in the eighteenth and the nineteenth centuries, it became possible to portray an actual dagger so that what had been a metaphor became stage business. Recently the tendency has been for the dagger to be a metaphor again, though Polanski's film does have a visible apparition of a dagger that eventually marshals Macbeth the way that he was going (line 43). In Jeremy Freeston's 1996–97 television film version, Jason Connery's Macbeth sees the shadow of an altar cross on the floor as light comes through a window behind it, and he speaks these lines while looking at the shadow.

tracks 19-21

34–65:
Simon Russell Beale as Macbeth
Ben Greet as Macbeth

37: **fatal vision:** apparition that is both fatal and fateful
43: **marshal'st:** leads, though probably with the secondary meaning of points
45–46: **Mine eyes are made the fools o' th' other senses, / Or else worth all the rest:** either my eyes have tricked all my other senses or only my eyes are telling me the truth
47: **dudgeon:** wooden handle; **gouts:** drops
50–51: **the one-half world / Nature seems dead:** the half of the globe where it is now night
53: **Pale Hecate:** goddess of the underworld; although represented in Greek myth as the daughter of the Titan Perses and of Asteria, in European witch lore she was seen as the patron or ruler of witches. She appears in this play in 3.5, as the crew chief of the weird sisters.
54: **Alarumed:** called to action
55: **whose howl's his watch:** the wolf, as the watchman, warns with his howl
56: **Tarquin:** Sextus Tarquinius, the Roman king, who raped the chaste Lucretia. Shakespeare tells the story in his poem "The Rape of Lucrece" (1594); **strides:** "sides" in the First Folio
57: **sure:** "sowre" in the First Folio
58: **way they:** "they may" in the First Folio
59: **prate:** talk too much, gossip; for the stones to do so would "take the present horror" from the situation, as he says in the next line
62: **Words...gives:** talking too much cools off the heated desire to act
62: Stage Direction: *A bell rings:* In 1788 Kemble had a clock strike rather than a bell ring. Some modern productions omit the sound effect and the last two and one-half lines.

Is this a dagger which I see before me,
The handle toward my hand? Come, let me clutch thee.   35
I have thee not, and yet I see thee still.
Art thou not, fatal vision, sensible
To feeling as to sight? Or art thou but
A dagger of the mind, a false creation,
Proceeding from the heat-oppressèd brain?   40
I see thee yet, in form as palpable
As this which now I draw.
Thou marshal'st me the way that I was going,
And such an instrument I was to use.
Mine eyes are made the fools o' th' other senses,   45
Or else worth all the rest. I see thee still,
And on thy blade and dudgeon gouts of blood,
Which was not so before. There's no such thing.
It is the bloody business which informs
Thus to mine eyes. Now o'er the one-half world   50
Nature seems dead, and wicked dreams abuse
The curtained sleep. Witchcraft celebrates
Pale Hecate's offerings, and withered Murder,
Alarumed by his sentinel, the wolf,
Whose howl's his watch, thus with his stealthy pace,   55
With Tarquin's ravishing [strides], towards his design
Moves like a ghost. Thou [sure] and firm-set earth,
Hear not my steps, which [way they] walk, for fear
Thy very stones prate of my whereabouts
And take the present horror from the time,   60
Which now suits with it. Whiles I threat, he lives.
Words to the heat of deeds too cold breath gives.

A bell rings

I go, and it is done. The bell invites me.
Hear it not, Duncan, for it is a knell
That summons thee to heaven or to hell.   65
                                                                                                                      Exit

3–5: Scene: *Hark...goodnight*: There is no direction indicating what sort of sound, if any, is to be heard here. Presumably it should be some sort of bird sound, but directors have had a number of sounds including Macbeth shouting, since he shouts from within at line 9.

4: bellman: originally the person who announced deaths and called on the faithful to pray for the souls of the departed; later on, the night watchman who rang the hours during the night

6: surfeited: fed to excess

7: possets: warm milky drinks

13: He: Macbeth; **he:** Duncan

14: Stage Direction: *Enter MACBETH*: McKellen (RSC, 1976) entered holding the daggers in front of him in full view of Dench. There they remained until line 50 when she noticed them for the first time. Pertwee (ESC, 1997) carries the daggers in his left hand beside his leg and Greta Scacchi stands so close to him that she does not see them until he raises them in gesture at lines 48–49. Sher (RSC,1999) enters with the daggers held behind his back and displays only one bloody hand at a time and only at lines 48–49 as Harriet Walter pushes him away to wash his hands does she see the daggers behind his back. Generally, however, the daggers are just not seen by Lady Macbeth no matter how Macbeth carries them.

15: My husband: the only time Lady Macbeth calls Macbeth "husband" in the entire play, and here, it is a question

16: "I have done the deed. Didst thou not hear a noise?": Jack Carter as Macbeth and Edna Thomas as Lady Macbeth in the 1936 production at the New Lafayette Theatre directed by Orson Welles

Library of Congress, Music Division, Federal Theatre Project Collection

Act 2, Scene 2]

LADY MACBETH
  That which hath made them drunk hath made me bold;
  What hath quenched them hath given me fire.
  Hark! Peace!
  It was the owl that shrieked, the fatal bellman,
  Which gives the stern'st goodnight. He is about it.   5
  The doors are open, and the surfeited grooms
  Do mock their charge with snores. I have drugged their possets,
  That death and nature do contend about them,
  Whether they live or die.

MACBETH [*Within*]
                    Who's there? What, ho!

LADY MACBETH
  Alack, I am afraid they have awaked,   10
  And 'tis not done. The attempt and not the deed
  Confounds us. Hark! I laid their daggers ready;
  He could not miss 'em. Had he not resembled
  My father as he slept, I had done't.

                                        Enter MACBETH
  My husband?   15

MACBETH
  I have done the deed. Didst thou not hear a noise?

LADY MACBETH
  I heard the owl scream and the crickets cry.
  Did not you speak?

MACBETH
                    When?

22: Scene: Conventionally, actors have looked at their hands holding the bloody daggers, but there is no such stage direction in the First Folio.

26: addressed them: applied themselves

29: As they: as if they

30: List'ning their: listening to their

Roger Allam as Macbeth and Brid Brennan as Lady Macbeth in the 1996 RSC production directed by Tim Albery

Photographer Reg Wilson © Royal Shakespeare Company

[THE SOURCEBOOKS SHAKESPEARE]   670–686

LADY MACBETH
                    Now.

MACBETH
                              As I descended?

LADY MACBETH
    Ay.

MACBETH
    Hark!—Who lies i' th' second chamber?   20

LADY MACBETH
    Donalbain.

MACBETH
    This is a sorry sight.

LADY MACBETH
    A foolish thought, to say a sorry sight.

MACBETH
    There's one did laugh in's sleep, and one cried "Murder!"
    That they did wake each other. I stood and heard them.   25
    But they did say their prayers, and addressed them
    Again to sleep.

LADY MACBETH
                    There are two lodged together.

MACBETH
    One cried "God bless us!" and "Amen" the other,
    As they had seen me with these hangman's hands.
    List'ning their fear, I could not say "Amen,"   30
    When they did say "God bless us!"

LADY MACBETH
    Consider it not so deeply.

36: **so:** if so

tracks 22-24

37–76:
Fay Bainter as Lady Macbeth and Orson Welles as Macbeth
Arthur Bourchier as Macbeth

39: **raveled:** unraveled

41: **second course:** second course and therefore the main course

44–45: "Glamis hath murdered sleep, and therefore Cawdor / Shall sleep no more. Macbeth shall sleep no more": Sir Derek Jacobi as Macbeth and Cheryl Campbell as Lady Macbeth in the 1993 RSC production directed by Adrian Noble
Photo: Donald Cooper

47: **unbend:** weaken or slacken

48: **brainsickly:** madly, with the additional sense of being ill

49: **filthy witness:** i.e., blood

MACBETH

But wherefore could not I pronounce "Amen"?
I had most need of blessing, and "Amen"
Stuck in my throat.

LADY MACBETH

These deeds must not be thought   35
After these ways; so, it will make us mad.

MACBETH

Methought I heard a voice cry "Sleep no more!
Macbeth does murder sleep," the innocent sleep,
Sleep that knits up the raveled sleeve of care,
The death of each day's life, sore labor's bath,   40
Balm of hurt minds, great nature's second course,
Chief nourisher in life's feast.

LADY MACBETH

What do you mean?

MACBETH

Still it cried "Sleep no more!" to all the house.
"Glamis hath murdered sleep, and therefore Cawdor
Shall sleep no more. Macbeth shall sleep no more."   45

LADY MACBETH

Who was it that thus cried? Why, worthy thane,
You do unbend your noble strength to think
So brainsickly of things. Go get some water,
And wash this filthy witness from your hand.
Why did you bring these daggers from the place?   50
They must lie there. Go, carry them and smear
The sleepy grooms with blood.

MACBETH

I'll go no more.
I am afraid to think what I have done.
Look on't again I dare not.

37–76:
Fay Bainter as Lady Macbeth and Orson Welles as Macbeth
Arthur Bourchier as Macbeth

54: **Infirm:** not steadfast, weak

58: **gild:** smear with blood, though since the blood is Duncan's royal blood, there is a secondary meaning of "covering with gold"; also, a pun on "guilt" in the next line

59: Stage Direction: First Folio reads only "*Knocke within*" and only "*Knocke*" at lines 67, 71, and 75; however, Macbeth's next words indicate that this is more than a single knock and that they are all offstage (within).

59: Scene: The knocking here and at lines 67, 71, and 75, should have the effect of startling Macbeth, and Lady Macbeth at the second occurrence, from the intense emotions which have built up during this scene. Thus the knocking must be loud, as might be heard on a castle gate.

64: **multitudinous:** innumerable, endless; **incarnadine:** turn the color of blood

70: **constancy:** firmness of purpose or intense concentration

71: **left you unattended:** abandoned you

72: **nightgown:** dressing gown

73: **watchers:** still awake

74: **poorly:** pointlessly

LADY MACBETH
                    Infirm of purpose!
Give me the daggers. The sleeping and the dead   55
Are but as pictures. 'Tis the eye of childhood
That fears a painted devil. If he do bleed,
I'll gild the faces of the grooms withal,
For it must seem their guilt.

Exit. Knock[ing] within.

MACBETH
                    Whence is that knocking?
How is't with me, when every noise appals me?   60
What hands are here? Ha! They pluck out mine eyes.
Will all great Neptune's ocean wash this blood
Clean from my hand? No, this my hand will rather
The multitudinous seas incarnadine,
Making the green one red.   65

Re-enter LADY MACBETH

LADY MACBETH
My hands are of your color, but I shame
To wear a heart so white.

Knock[ing within]

                    I hear a knocking
At the south entry. Retire we to our chamber.
A little water clears us of this deed.
How easy is it, then! Your constancy   70
Hath left you unattended.

Knock[ing within]

                    Hark, more knocking.
Get on your nightgown, lest occasion call us,
And show us to be watchers. Be not lost
So poorly in your thoughts.

MACBETH
To know my deed, 'twere best not know myself.   75

Knock[ing within]

Wake Duncan with thy knocking! I would thou couldst!

Exeunt

0: Stage Direction: ***porter***: one who has charge of a door or gate, particularly of a fortified house or castle

1–34: Scene: Davenant (1664) cut the porter from the play and he stayed out of the play until Phelps restored a part of him in 1844. In the last one hundred years the porter's speeches have finally been fully restored.

tracks 25-26

1–36:
David Tennant as the Porter and Gary Bakewell as Macduff

2: **have old:** have enough of or grow old in the work of

3: **Beelzebub:** according to Matthew 12:24, he is the prince of the devils

4: **Here's a farmer...expectation of plenty:** farmers are legendary for anticipating good crops and always thinking they have had poor ones

5: **Come in time:** you're just in time; **enow:** enough

7: **equivocator:** one who uses words in more than one sense or uses words with a double meaning. As Macbeth will learn, the witches are equivocators.

7–8: **swear in both the scales against / either scale:** give testimony under oath on either side of a question

8: **committed treason enough for God's sake:** gave false testimony allegedly for religious reasons

11: **stealing out of a French hose:** skimping on material in the making of French hose, which were very tight-fitting

12: **roast your goose:** a goose is a long-handled tailor's iron that he can heat in hell

15–16: **the primrose way to the / everlasting bonfire:** the path of pleasure that leads to hell

21: **till the second cock:** until the second crowing of the cock, near daybreak

Act 2, Scene 3]

Enter a porter. Knocking within.

Porter
Here's a knocking indeed. If a man were porter of hell gate, he
should have old turning the key.

Knock[ing within]

Knock, knock, knock! Who's there, i' th' name of Beelzebub?
Here's a farmer, that hanged himself on th' expectation of plenty.
Come in time, have napkins enow about you, here you'll sweat for't.   5

Knock[ing within]

Knock, knock! Who's there, in the other devil's name? Faith,
here's an equivocator, that could swear in both the scales against
either scale, who committed treason enough for God's sake, yet
could not equivocate to heaven. O, come in, equivocator.

Knock[ing within]

Knock, knock, knock! Who's there? Faith, here's an English tai-   10
lor come hither, for stealing out of a French hose. Come in tailor,
here you may roast your goose.

Knock[ing within]

Knock, knock, never at quiet! What are you? But this place is too
cold for hell. I'll devil-porter it no further. I had thought to have
let in some of all professions that go the primrose way to the   15
everlasting bonfire.

Knock[ing within]

Anon, anon!

Enter MACDUFF and LENNOX

I pray you, remember the porter.

MACDUFF
Was it so late, friend, ere you went to bed,
That you do lie so late?   20

Porter
Faith sir, we were carousing till the second cock, and drink, sir, is
a great provoker of three things.

1–36:
David Tennant as the Porter and Gary Bakewell as Macduff

24: **nose-painting:** making the nose red through heavy drinking

30: **giving him the lie:** lying directly; also a pun on lying down drunk

32: **very throat on me:** to "give one the lie in the throat" was to accuse someone of lying; there is also an association between the throat and drinking

33–34: **took up my / legs:** caused me to fall down

34: **cast him:** either urinate or throw up on him

The Porter from the 1936 production at the New Lafayette Theatre directed by Orson Welles

Library of Congress, Music Division, Federal Theatre Project Collection

35: Stage Direction: ***Enter MACBETH:*** Macbeth's costume when entering has changed from gigantic nightrobes (Macready) to pajamas, but in whatever attire he enters it should appear that he has just arisen from sleep, as indeed should most of the others who now enter.

MACDUFF
What three things does drink especially provoke?

Porter
Marry, sir, nose-painting, sleep, and urine. Lechery, sir, it provokes,
and unprovokes; it provokes the desire, but it takes away the per-   25
formance. Therefore, much drink may be said to be an equivocator
with lechery. It makes him, and it mars him; it sets him on, and it
takes him off; it persuades him, and disheartens him; makes him
stand to, and not stand to; in conclusion, equivocates him in a sleep,
and, giving him the lie, leaves him.   30

MACDUFF
I believe drink gave thee the lie last night.

Porter
That it did, sir, i' the very throat on me; but I requited him for his
lie, and, I think, being too strong for him, though he took up my
legs sometime, yet I made a shift to cast him.

MACDUFF
Is thy master stirring?   35
Enter MACBETH

Our knocking has awaked him, here he comes.

[Exit porter]

LENNOX
Good morrow, noble sir.

MACBETH
                    Good morrow, both.

MACDUFF
Is the king stirring, worthy thane?

MACBETH
                    Not yet.

39: **timely:** early

40: **slipped:** missed

43: **physics:** treats or cures

45: **limited service:** appointed duty

47: **appoint so:** plan to

48: **unruly:** turbulent, tempestuous

52: **combustion:** tumult or destruction

53: **obscure bird:** owl (obscure = living in the dark)

Costume rendering for Macduff from the 1937 production at the Old Vic directed by Michel Saint-Denis

Rare Book and Special Collections Library, University of Illinois at Urbana-Champaign

MACDUFF

He did command me to call timely on him.
I have almost slipped the hour.

MACBETH

           I'll bring you to him.   40

MACDUFF

I know this is a joyful trouble to you,
But yet 'tis one.

MACBETH

The labor we delight in physics pain.
This is the door.

MACDUFF

          I'll make so bold to call,
For 'tis my limited service.   45

Exit

LENNOX

Goes the king hence today?

MACBETH

He does. He did appoint so.

LENNOX

The night has been unruly. Where we lay,
Our chimneys were blown down, and, as they say,
Lamentings heard i' th' air, strange screams of death,   50
And prophesying with accents terrible
Of dire combustion and confused events
New hatched to the woeful time. The obscure bird
Clamored the livelong night. Some say, the earth
Was feverous and did shake.

MACBETH

         Twas a rough night.   55

60: Confusion: destruction

62: Lord's anointed temple: Duncan's body (the king was seen as the Lord's anointed)

66: Gorgon: mythological creature, the sight of which killed instantly

70: downy: placid, soft

72: great doom's image: representation of Doomsday

73: As...sprites: as spirits risen from their graves on Doomsday

74: Ring the bell: some editions omit these words from the First Folio, arguing that they are a prompter's note that has mistakenly been included in the printed text. As the case for this does not seem conclusive, the words have been retained.

Costume rendering for Lennox from the 1937 production at the Old Vic directed by Michel Saint-Denis

Rare Book and Special Collections Library, University of Illinois at Urbana-Champaign

LENNOX
My young remembrance cannot parallel
A fellow to it.

Re-enter MACDUFF

MACDUFF
O horror, horror, horror!
Tongue nor heart cannot conceive nor name thee!

MACBETH *and* LENNOX
What's the matter?

MACDUFF
Confusion now hath made his masterpiece!   60
Most sacrilegious murder hath broke ope
The Lord's anointed temple, and stole thence
The life o' th' building!

MACBETH
What is't you say, the life?

LENNOX
Mean you his majesty?

MACDUFF
Approach the chamber, and destroy your sight   65
With a new Gorgon. Do not bid me speak.
See, and then speak yourselves. Awake, awake!
Exeunt MACBETH and LENNOX
Ring the alarum-bell. Murder and treason!
Banquo and Donalbain, Malcolm, awake!
Shake off this downy sleep, death's counterfeit,   70
And look on death itself. Up, up, and see
The great doom's image. Malcolm, Banquo,
As from your graves rise up and walk like sprites,
To countenance this horror. Ring the bell!

Bell rings
Enter LADY [MACBETH]

76: trumpet calls to parley: Lady Macbeth thinks of the alarm bell as a trumpet calling military leaders to a conference (parley)

83: Duff: this shortening of Macduff's name occurs only this one time in the play

83: prithee: pray thee

85–86: "Had I but died an hour before this chance, / I had lived a blessèd time": the Ensemble in the Shakespeare Theatre Company's 2004–05 production directed by Michael Kahn
Photo: Richard Termine

88: toys: trifles; **grace:** honor

89: lees: dregs

90: vault: wine cellar, but also an allusion to the vault of the heavens: the world

91: amiss: wrong

LADY MACBETH
What's the business, 75
That such a hideous trumpet calls to parley
The sleepers of the house? Speak, speak!

MACDUFF
O gentle lady,
'Tis not for you to hear what I can speak.
The repetition, in a woman's ear,
Would murder as it fell. O Banquo, Banquo, 80
Enter BANQUO

Our royal master's murdered!

LADY MACBETH
Woe, alas!
What, in our house?

BANQUO
Too cruel anywhere.
Dear Duff, I prithee, contradict thyself,
And say it is not so.
Re-enter MACBETH, LENNOX, and ROSS

MACBETH
Had I but died an hour before this chance, 85
I had lived a blessèd time; for from this instant
There's nothing serious in mortality.
All is but toys. Renown and grace is dead.
The wine of life is drawn, and the mere lees
Is left this vault to brag of. 90
Enter MALCOLM and DONALBAIN

DONALBAIN
What is amiss?

MACBETH
You are, and do not know't
The spring, the head, the fountain of your blood
Is stopped, the very source of it is stopped.

96: **badged:** marked with blood as a badge of murder

98: **distracted:** bewildered or stunned out of one's wits

101: **Wherefore:** why

104: **expedition:** speed

107: **a breach:** an opening broken in a wall of defense

110: **Unmannerly:** inappropriately, improperly; **breeched:** clothed in blood; literally, dressed in breeches of blood

112: **make's:** make his

112: "Help me hence, ho!": Cheryl Campbell as Lady Macbeth attended by ladies in the 1993 RSC production directed by Adrian Noble
Photo: Donald Cooper

MACDUFF
    Your royal father's murdered.

MALCOLM
                    O, by whom?

LENNOX
    Those of his chamber, as it seemed, had done't.   95
    Their hands and faces were all badged with blood;
    So were their daggers, which unwiped we found
    Upon their pillows. They stared, and were distracted.
    No man's life was to be trusted with them.

MACBETH
    O, yet I do repent me of my fury,   100
    That I did kill them.

MACDUFF
                    Wherefore did you so?

MACBETH
    Who can be wise, amazed, temp'rate and furious,
    Loyal and neutral, in a moment? No man.
    Th' expedition my violent love
    Outrun the pauser, reason. Here lay Duncan,   105
    His silver skin laced with his golden blood;
    And his gashed stabs looked like a breach in nature
    For ruin's wasteful entrance. There the murderers,
    Steeped in the colors of their trade, their daggers
    Unmannerly breeched with gore. Who could refrain   110
    That had a heart to love, and in that heart
    Courage to make's love known?

LADY MACBETH
                    Help me hence, ho!

MACDUFF
    Look to the lady.

116: **auger-hole:** hole made by an auger drill bit; hence, a small hole

117: **brewed:** created; they have not yet been seen to weep

118: **Nor our strong sorrow upon the foot of motion:** our great sorrow will disguise our readiness to move

120: **we have our naked frailties hid:** we are dressed in our daytime clothes

122: **question:** examine

123: **scruples:** doubts or suspicions

125: **undivulged pretense:** secret purposes

127: **briefly:** quickly; **manly readiness:** proper clothing

128: **contented:** agreed

MALCOLM

> [*Aside to Donalbain*] Why do we hold our tongues,
That most may claim this argument for ours?

DONALBAIN

[*Aside to Malcolm*] What should be spoken here, where our fate,   115
Hid in an auger-hole, may rush and seize us?
Let's away. Our tears are not yet brewed.

MALCOLM

[*Aside to Donalbain*] Nor our strong sorrow upon the foot of motion.

BANQUO

Look to the lady.

> [*LADY MACBETH is carried out*]

And when we have our naked frailties hid,   120
That suffer in exposure, let us meet
And question this most bloody piece of work
To know it further. Fears and scruples shake us.
In the great hand of God I stand, and thence
Against the undivulged pretense I fight   125
Of treasonous malice.

MACDUFF

> And so do I.

All

> So all.

MACBETH

Let's briefly put on manly readiness,
And meet i' th' hall together.

All

> Well contented.
> *Exeunt. [Manet MALCOLM and DONALBAIN.]*

129: **consort:** join

134–135: **The near in blood, / The nearer bloody:** Donalbain is warning Malcolm that they might be killed next, since they are Duncan's sons

136: **lighted:** landed

138: **dainty:** too polite

139: **shift away:** slip away secretly; **warrant:** rightness, legality

Costume rendering for Donalbain from the 1937 production at the Old Vic directed by Michel Saint-Denis
Rare Book and Special Collections Library, University of Illinois at Urbana-Champaign

MALCOLM

    What will you do? Let's not consort with them.
    To show an unfelt sorrow is an office   130
    Which the false man does easy. I'll to England.

DONALBAIN

    To Ireland, I. Our separated fortune
    Shall keep us both the safer. Where we are
    There's daggers in men's smiles. The near in blood,
    The nearer bloody.

MALCOLM

                 This murderous shaft that's shot   135
    Hath not yet lighted, and our safest way
    Is to avoid the aim. Therefore, to horse,
    And let us not be dainty of leave-taking,
    But shift away. There's warrant in that theft
    Which steals itself, when there's no mercy left.   140
                                Exeunt

0: **Scene:** Although this scene has frequently been cut, it provides what one might call commentary on the situation in Scotland and its manifestation in the physical world. If the Old Man's statement in line 1 is to be taken seriously, he must be played as a very old man indeed.

1: **Threescore and ten:** seventy years; the biblical life span of man according to Psalms 90:10, "The days of our years are threescore years and ten"

2–3: "I have seen / Hours dreadful and things strange": Leon Addison Brown as the Old Man in The Shakespeare Theatre of New Jersey's 2004 production directed by Bonnie J. Monte

Photo: Gerry Goodstein

3: **sore:** dreadful

4: **trifled:** trivialized; **former knowings:** previous experiences

5–10: **Thou seest...kiss it:** Ross is describing the darkness of the day and how that fits with the mood of the country

7: **the travailing lamp:** the sun (lamp) moving with great difficulty (travailing); although most editions modernize "travailing" to "traveling," this change doesn't seem to convey the full meaning of the original reading

12: **pride of place:** peak of flight

13: **mousing owl:** referencing that mice are common prey of owls; **hawked:** attacked

15: **minions:** especially favored ones

16: **flung out:** lunged

17: **Contending:** fighting

17–18: **make / War with mankind:** attack their handlers

Act 2, Scene 4]

OLD MAN
  Threescore and ten I can remember well,
  Within the volume of which time I have seen
  Hours dreadful and things strange; but this sore night
  Hath trifled former knowings.

ROSS
             Ha, good father,
  Thou seest the heavens, as troubled with man's act,   5
  Threaten his bloody stage. By th' clock,' tis day,
  And yet dark night strangles the travailing lamp.
  Is't night's predominance or the day's shame
  That darkness does the face of earth entomb
  When living light should kiss it?

OLD MAN
           'Tis unnatural   10
  Even like the deed that's done. On Tuesday last,
  A falcon, towering in her pride of place,
  Was by a mousing owl hawked at and killed.

ROSS
  And Duncan's horses (a thing most strange and certain),
  Beauteous and swift, the minions of their race,   15
  Turned wild in nature, broke their stalls, flung out,
  Contending 'gainst obedience, as they would make
  War with mankind.

OLD MAN
         'Tis said they eat each other.

24: **good:** benefit; **pretend:** imagine, **suborned:** secretly bribed

27: **'Gainst nature:** unnatural (since they plotted the death of their father)

28: **Thriftless:** profitless; **ravin up:** eat greedily

29: **Thine own life's means:** the source of one's own existence

31: **Scone:** near Perth, it is where Scotland's kings were traditionally crowned

32: **invested:** crowned and clothed in his robes of state

ROSS

They did so, to the amazement of mine eyes
That looked upon't.

Enter MACDUFF

Here comes the good Macduff.   20
How goes the world, sir, now?

MACDUFF

Why, see you not?

ROSS

Is't known who did this more than bloody deed?

MACDUFF

Those that Macbeth hath slain.

ROSS

Alas, the day,
What good could they pretend?

MACDUFF

They were suborned.
Malcolm and Donalbain, the king's two sons,   25
Are stol'n away and fled, which puts upon them
Suspicion of the deed.

ROSS

'Gainst nature still!
Thriftless ambition, that wilt ravin up
Thine own life's means! Then 'tis most like
The sovereignty will fall upon Macbeth.   30

MACDUFF

He is already named and gone to Scone
To be invested.

ROSS

Where is Duncan's body?

33: Colmekill: a small island off the end of the Ross of Mull peninsula on the west coast of Scotland where Scottish kings were usually buried; it is now called Iona

36: Fife: Macduff's home and castle; **thither:** to that place (Scone)

38: Lest: for fear that

40: benison: blessing

42: Scene: Trevor Nunn as well as Michael Kahn (in the Shakespeare Theatre Company's 2004–05 production) inserted the ceremony of Macbeth's coronation between this scene and the next.

Kelly McGillis as Lady Macbeth and Patrick Page as Macbeth with the Ensemble in the Shakespeare Theatre Company's 2004–05 production directed by Michael Kahn
Photo: Richard Termine

MACDUFF
  Carried to Colmekill,
  The sacred storehouse of his predecessors,
  And guardian of their bones.

ROSS
                 Will you to Scone?   35

MACDUFF
  No, cousin, I'll to Fife.

ROSS
                 Well, I will thither.

MACDUFF
  Well, may you see things well done there. Adieu,
  Lest our old robes sit easier than our new.

                                        [Exit MACDUFF]

ROSS
  Farewell, father.

OLD MAN
  God's benison go with you,   *[Exit ROSS]*
                 and with those   40
  That would make good of bad and friends of foes.

                                        [Exit OLD MAN]

[Macbeth

Act 3

1–10: Scene: This scene seems to be set in an anteroom apart from the main hall. On the Globe stage, this could be done by having Banquo on the outer edge of the stage to the side of a stage post.

The coronation of Macbeth occurs outside the play, between acts 2 and 3. In Polanski's film, Martin Shaw's Banquo delivers his ten-line speech as a voice-over to the coronation.
Courtesy: Douglas Lanier

4: **stand:** continue

10: Stage Direction: *Sennet*: a trumpet flourish, normally announcing a formal entrance

10: Stage Direction: *as king*: This is an indication that Macbeth should enter in robes of state and probably be crowned. Although the First Folio only says "Lady" for Lady Macbeth's entrance, we must assume that she would be similarly attired.

13: **all-thing:** entirely

14: **solemn supper:** formal banquet

14–39: Scene: These lines, or at least the latter part of them, are spoken exclusively between Macbeth and Banquo and the former does not again address the entire assembly, including Lady Macbeth, until line 40. To achieve this on any stage, they must walk apart, probably downstage, as they speak.

16: **Command upon me:** a royal summons (contrast with Macbeth's "request" in the previous line)

Act 3, Scene 1]

Enter BANQUO

BANQUO
 Thou hast it now—king, Cawdor, Glamis, all
 As the weird women promised, and I fear,
 Thou played'st most foully for't. Yet it was said
 It should not stand in thy posterity,
 But that myself should be the root and father   5
 Of many kings. If there come truth from them—
 As upon thee, Macbeth, their speeches shine—
 Why, by the verities on thee made good,
 May they not be my oracles as well
 And set me up in hope? But hush, no more.   10
 Sennet sounded. Enter MACBETH, as king,
 LADY [MACBETH, as queen], LENNOX,
 ROSS, LORDS, and attendants.

MACBETH
 Here's our chief guest.

LADY MACBETH
                    If he had been forgotten,
 It had been as a gap in our great feast
 And all-thing unbecoming.

MACBETH
 Tonight we hold a solemn supper, sir,
 And I'll request your presence.

BANQUO
                    Let your highness   15
 Command upon me, to the which my duties
 Are with a most indissoluble tie
 Forever knit.

21: **still:** always; **prosperous:** useful

22: **take:** take it, i.e., have your advice

25–27: **Go not my horse . . . a dark hour or twain:** if my horse doesn't go fast enough I won't be back until an hour or two after dark (twain = two)

29: **bloody cousins:** refers to Malcolm and Donalbain; **bestowed:** lodged

32: **strange:** remarkable, extraordinary; **invention:** falsehood

33: **therewithal:** with that, at the same time; **cause of state:** affairs of state

34: **Craving us jointly:** requiring both of our attention

36: **Our time does call upon's:** i.e., we need to leave now

MACBETH
          Ride you this afternoon?

BANQUO
  Ay, my good lord.

MACBETH
  We should have else desired your good advice,   20
  Which still hath been both grave and prosperous,
  In this day's council, but we'll take tomorrow.
  Is't far you ride?

BANQUO
  As far, my lord, as will fill up the time
  'Twixt this and supper. Go not my horse the better,   25
  I must become a borrower of the night
  For a dark hour or twain.

MACBETH
          Fail not our feast.

BANQUO
  My lord, I will not.

MACBETH
  We hear, our bloody cousins are bestowed
  In England and in Ireland, not confessing   30
  Their cruel parricide, filling their hearers
  With strange invention. But of that tomorrow,
  When therewithal we shall have cause of state
  Craving us jointly. Hie you to horse. Adieu,
  Till you return at night. Goes Fleance with you?   35

BANQUO
  Ay, my good lord. Our time does call upon's.

MACBETH
  I wish your horses swift and sure of foot;
  And so I do commend you to their backs.
  Farewell.

                                    Exit BANQUO

43: Scene: *alone:* This can be used, and has been, notably by Bogdanov, to dismiss not only the other members of the Court but Lady Macbeth as well. Indeed, the following "God be with you" was used by McKellen to enforce her dismissal.

44: **Sirrah:** term addressed to males expressing contempt, reprimand, or the assumption of authority by the speaker

47–71:
Alec Guinness as Macbeth
Stephen Dillane as Macbeth

47–71: Scene: *To be thus . . . utterance:* The stage directions in the First Folio and in all modern editions have Macbeth deliver this speech as a soliloquy, alone on stage. However, not every modern production does so. For example, Polanski has Macbeth deliver these lines to Lady Macbeth through line 55, after which he delivers the balance as a soliloquy.

49: **Stick deep:** are deeply rooted; **royalty of nature:** naturally royal conduct
51: **dauntless temper of his mind:** fearless temperament
55: **genius is rebuked:** guiding nature is reproached
56: **Caesar:** Octavius Caesar, later known as the Emperor Augustus.
See Shakespeare's *Antony and Cleopatra* (2.3).
60: **fruitless:** literally "without offspring," but here it means "without offspring to succeed me"
62: **an unlineal hand:** someone not directly descended from the family line
64: **filed:** defiled
66: **rancors:** ill will
67: **eternal jewel:** soul
68: **common enemy of man:** i.e., the devil
70: **list:** usually "lists," the jousting field in tournaments
71: **champion:** oppose; **th' utterance:** the utmost
71: Scene: Macbeth's sudden "Who's there?" indicates how deeply he has become involved in his soliloquy—he seems to have forgotten he has sent for these men.

Let every man be master of his time   40
Till seven at night. To make society
The sweeter welcome, we will keep ourself
Till suppertime alone. While then, God be with you.
                    Exeunt. Manet MACBETH and a servant.
Sirrah, a word with you. Attend those men
Our pleasure?   45

Servant
They are, my lord, without the palace gate.

MACBETH
Bring them before us.
                                                    Exit servant

                    To be thus is nothing,
But to be safely thus. Our fears in Banquo
Stick deep, and in his royalty of nature
Reigns that which would be feared. 'Tis much he dares,   50
And to that dauntless temper of his mind
He hath a wisdom that doth guide his valor
To act in safety. There is none but he
Whose being I do fear; and under him
My genius is rebuked, as it is said   55
Mark Antony's was by Caesar. He chid the sisters
When first they put the name of king upon me,
And bade them speak to him. Then prophet-like
They hailed him father to a line of kings;
Upon my head they placed a fruitless crown   60
And put a barren scepter in my grip,
Thence to be wrenched with an unlineal hand,
No son of mine succeeding. If't be so,
For Banquo's issue have I filed my mind;
For them the gracious Duncan have I murdered;   65
Put rancors in the vessel of my peace
Only for them, and mine eternal jewel
Given to the common enemy of man
To make them kings, the seed of Banquo kings.
Rather than so, come fate into the list   70
And champion me to th' utterance. Who's there?

71: Stage Direction: ***Murderers***: Although this is what they are called in the First Folio, there seems nothing to indicate that they are already killers rather than just being poor, unfortunate men willing to do almost anything to survive.

Laurence Olivier as Macbeth delivering his soliloquy in the 1955 RSC production directed by Glen Byam Shaw

Photographer Angus McBean © Royal Shakespeare Company

72: Scene: This line is directed only to the servant. One assumes that there will follow a slight pause while the servant exits before he begins to address the Murderers in the next line.

76–77: **held you / So under fortune:** kept you poor or unfortunate

79: **passed in probation with you:** proved to you

80: **borne in hand:** deceived; **crossed:** thwarted; **instruments:** means (legal actions and also "agents," because of what follows)

81: **Who wrought with them:** either who executed the actions for Banquo, or with whom Banquo dealt in taking the actions

82: **half a soul:** half-wit; **notion crazed:** mad mind

87: **gospelled:** religious, ruled by the Gospels

90: **beggared:** reduced to beggary; **yours:** your heirs

91: **catalogue:** list of human types

93: **Shoughs:** lap dogs; **water-rugs:** water spaniels; **demi-wolves:** perhaps a crossbreed of wolf and domesticated dog; **clept:** called

Re-enter servant with two MURDERERS
Now go to the door, and stay there till we call.

Exit servant

Was it not yesterday we spoke together?

Murderers
It was, so please your highness.

MACBETH
                    Well then, now
Have you considered of my speeches? Know   75
That it was he in the times past which held you
So under fortune, which you thought had been
Our innocent self. This I made good to you
In our last conference, passed in probation with you,
How you were borne in hand, how crossed, the instruments,   80
Who wrought with them, and all things else that might
To half a soul and to a notion crazed
Say "Thus did Banquo."

FIRST MURDERER
                    You made it known to us.

MACBETH
I did so, and went further, which is now
Our point of second meeting. Do you find   85
Your patience so predominant in your nature
That you can let this go? Are you so gospelled
To pray for this good man and for his issue,
Whose heavy hand hath bowed you to the grave
And beggared yours forever?

FIRST MURDERER
                    We are men, my liege.   90

MACBETH
Ay, in the catalogue ye go for men,
As hounds and greyhounds, mongrels, spaniels, curs,
Shoughs, water-rugs and demi-wolves, are clept

94: valued file: list of dogs' values or abilities

96: housekeeper: watchdog

99: Particular addition: special characteristics; **bill:** list of traits

100: all alike: merely dogs

101: station in the file: particular rank among men

106: in his life: because Banquo is alive

107: perfect: completely contented

111: tugged with: pulled around by

113–114: "Both of you / Know Banquo was your enemy": Jon Finch as Macbeth, Michael Balfour as First Murderer, and Andrew McCulloch as Second Murderer in *The Tragedy of Macbeth* (1971) directed by Roman Polanski
Courtesy: Douglas Lanier

115: bloody distance: dangerously close ("distance" is a technical term from fencing)

116: thrusts: thrusts his sword (fencing reference, as in line 115)

117: near'st of life: heart

All by the name of dogs. The valued file
Distinguishes the swift, the slow, the subtle,   95
The housekeeper, the hunter, every one
According to the gift which bounteous nature
Hath in him closed; whereby he does receive
Particular addition, from the bill
That writes them all alike. And so of men.   100
Now, if you have a station in the file,
Not i' th' worst rank of manhood, say't;
And I will put that business in your bosoms,
Whose execution takes your enemy off,
Grapples you to the heart and love of us,   105
Who wear out health but sickly in his life,
Which in his death were perfect.

SECOND MURDERER
     I am one, my liege,
Whom the vile blows and buffets of the world
Have so incensed that I am reckless what
I do to spite the world.

FIRST MURDERER
     And I another   110
So weary with disasters, tugged with fortune,
That I would set my life on any chance,
To mend it, or be rid on't.

MACBETH
    Both of you
Know Banquo was your enemy.

Murderers
    True, my lord.

MACBETH
So is he mine; and in such bloody distance,   115
That every minute of his being thrusts
Against my near'st of life. And though I could
With barefaced power sweep him from my sight

119: **avouch:** justify
120: **For:** because of
121–122: **wail his fall . . . struck down:** appear to weep for the murder I have arranged
123: **make love:** seek your help
127: **spirits:** natures, or characters
129: **perfect spy o'th' time:** exact details of the plan

130: "The moment on't, for't must be done tonight": Christopher Walken as Macbeth in the 1974 Public Theatre production directed by Edward Berkeley
Photo: George E. Joseph

130: **on't:** of it
131: **something from:** some way from; **always thought:** always bear in mind
132: **a clearness:** no connection with, an alibi
133: **rubs nor botches:** faults, flaws
137: **Resolve yourselves apart:** decide between you privately
139: **straight:** at once

And bid my will avouch it, yet I must not,
For certain friends that are both his and mine,   120
Whose loves I may not drop, but wail his fall
Who I myself struck down. And thence it is
That I to your assistance do make love,
Masking the business from the common eye
For sundry weighty reasons.

SECOND MURDERER
              We shall, my lord,   125
Perform what you command us.

FIRST MURDERER
              Though our lives—

MACBETH
Your spirits shine through you. Within this hour at most
I will advise you where to plant yourselves,
Acquaint you with the perfect spy o' th' time,
The moment on't, for't must be done tonight   130
And something from the palace; always thought
That I require a clearness. And with him,
To leave no rubs nor botches in the work,
Fleance his son, that keeps him company,
Whose absence is no less material to me   135
Than is his father's, must embrace the fate
Of that dark hour. Resolve yourselves apart.
I'll come to you anon.

Murderers
              We are resolved, my lord.

MACBETH
I'll call upon you straight. Abide within.
                             Exeunt MURDERERS
It is concluded. Banquo, thy soul's flight,   140
If it find heaven, must find it out tonight.
                                    Exit

0: Location: On the Globe stage, the scene would have just been another one on the same stage. In productions since 1660, there has been some attempt to make it another room in the castle.

0: Stage Direction: the First Folio actually reads "*Macbeths Lady*"

3: **attend his leisure:** (term of courtesy) be at his service

5: **Naught's had, all's spent:** we have gained nothing and wasted all our resources

10: **sorriest fancies:** depressing imaginings

12–13: **Things without all remedy / Should be without regard:** i.e., don't worry about things that can't be changed

14: **scorched:** slashed

15: **close:** heal; **poor malice:** weak evil

16: **her former tooth:** the snake's previous venom (before we scorched her)

17: **let the frame of things disjoint:** let the order of the universe collapse; **both the worlds suffer:** heaven and earth be destroyed

Matheson Lang as Macbeth and Hilda Britton as Lady Macbeth (1911)
Mary Evans Picture Library

Enter LADY MACBETH and a servant

LADY MACBETH
Is Banquo gone from court?

Servant
Ay, madam, but returns again tonight.

LADY MACBETH
Say to the king, I would attend his leisure
For a few words.

Servant
Madam, I will.

Exit [servant]

LADY MACBETH
Naught's had, all's spent,   5
Where our desire is got without content.
'Tis safer to be that which we destroy
Than by destruction dwell in doubtful joy.

Enter MACBETH

How now, my lord, why do you keep alone,
Of sorriest fancies your companions making,   10
Using those thoughts which should indeed have died
With them they think on? Things without all remedy
Should be without regard. What's done is done.

MACBETH
We have scorched the snake, not killed it.
She'll close and be herself, whilst our poor malice   15
Remains in danger of her former tooth.
But let the frame of things disjoint, both the worlds suffer,
Ere we will eat our meal in fear and sleep
In the affliction of these terrible dreams
That shake us nightly. Better be with the dead,   20

23: **restless ecstasy:** sleepless frenzy

26: **Malice domestic:** civil war or civil conspiracy; **levy:** armies

28: **Gentle:** calm down; **sleek o'er your rugged looks:** smooth over your furrowed brow

31: **Let your remembrance . . . Banquo:** don't forget Banquo

32: **Present him eminence, both with eye and tongue:** show special favor in both looks and speech

33: **Unsafe the while:** we are not safe during this period

33–34: **lave / Our honors:** wash our reputations

35: **vizards:** masks

36: **leave this:** stop talking in this way

39: **in them nature's copy's not eterne:** they are not immortal

42: **cloistered:** enclosed; this reference is probably to the cloisters and church buildings, which bats inhabit

43: **shard-born:** born in dung

44: **yawning peal:** the beetle's hums serve as curfew bell to announce the fall of night

44–45: **there shall be . . . dreadful note:** the first overt instance of Macbeth plotting without the assistance of Lady Macbeth

Whom we, to gain our peace, have sent to peace,
Than on the torture of the mind to lie
In restless ecstasy. Duncan is in his grave;
After life's fitful fever he sleeps well.
Treason has done his worst; nor steel, nor poison,   25
Malice domestic, foreign levy, nothing,
Can touch him further.

LADY MACBETH
                    Come on.
Gentle my lord, sleek o'er your rugged looks.
Be bright and jovial among your guests tonight.

MACBETH
So shall I, love, and so, I pray, be you.   30
Let your remembrance apply to Banquo;
Present him eminence, both with eye and tongue:
Unsafe the while, that we must lave
Our honors in these flattering streams
And make our faces vizards to our hearts,   35
Disguising what they are.

LADY MACBETH
                    You must leave this.

MACBETH
O, full of scorpions is my mind, dear wife.
Thou know'st that Banquo and his Fleance lives.

LADY MACBETH
But in them nature's copy's not eterne.

MACBETH
There's comfort yet; they are assailable.   40
Then be thou jocund. Ere the bat hath flown
His cloistered flight, ere to black Hecate's summons
The shard-born beetle with his drowsy hums
Hath rung night's yawning peal, there shall be done
A deed of dreadful note.

46: **chuck:** chick, a term of affection

47: **seeling:** blinding (term from falconry, meaning sewing up a hood to cover a falcon's head to keep it in darkness)

48: **Scarf up:** blindfold; **pitiful:** compassionate

50: **that great bond:** i.e., Banquo's life

52: **rooky wood:** Macbeth is probably thinking that the woods where crows nest are a kind of rookery, since rooks are a member of the crow family

Jack Carter as Macbeth and Edna Thomas as Lady Macbeth in the 1936 production at the New Lafayette Theatre directed by Orson Welles
Library of Congress, Music Division, Federal Theatre Project Collection

LADY MACBETH

              What's to be done?   45

MACBETH

  Be innocent of the knowledge, dearest chuck,
  Till thou applaud the deed. Come, seeling night,
  Scarf up the tender eye of pitiful day;
  And with thy bloody and invisible hand
  Cancel and tear to pieces that great bond   50
  Which keeps me pale. Light thickens, and the crow
  Makes wing to the rooky wood.
  Good things of day begin to droop and drowse,
  While night's black agents to their preys do rouse.
  Thou marvel'st at my words, but hold thee still.   55
  Things bad begun make strong themselves by ill.
  So, prithee go with me.

                                       Exeunt

0: Location: This scene at the Globe would, of course, have been on the main stage with the Murderers carrying torches to indicate that it is night. In modern productions, some attempt is usually made to make it appear that this is happening outside or nearby the castle. Macbeth has told the Murderers in 3.1.131 that it must be done "something from [some way from] the palace."

0: Stage Direction: *three:* There has been much discussion over the years about the identity and purpose of the Third Murderer. Some have argued that the Third Murderer is Macbeth in disguise, though nothing that Macbeth has said at the end of 3.1 indicates whether he will inform the Murderers of the time and place in person or through a servant. The Third Murderer does seem to know a little more about Banquo than do the other two (see lines 13–15). However, if Macbeth were the Third, there would be no need for him to be told of the results of the murder in the following scene.

Hecate was the Third Murderer in the 1936 production at the New Lafayette Theatre directed by Orson Welles

Library of Congress, Music Division, Federal Theatre Project Collection

2: **needs:** deserves

3: **offices:** duties, authority

4: **direction just:** precise instructions

6: **lated:** belated

7: **and:** the First Folio reads "end"

8: **subject of our watch:** person for whom we are looking

10–11: **The rest . . . of expectation:** those guests who are expected

12: **go about:** take an indirect route

Act 3, Scene 3]

FIRST MURDERER
But who did bid thee join with us?

THIRD MURDERER
      Macbeth.

SECOND MURDERER
He needs not our mistrust, since he delivers
Our offices and what we have to do
To the direction just.

FIRST MURDERER
      Then stand with us.
The west yet glimmers with some streaks of day.   5
Now spurs the lated traveler apace
To gain the timely inn, [and] near approaches
The subject of our watch.

THIRD MURDERER
      Hark, I hear horses.

BANQUO *within*
Give us a light there, ho!

SECOND MURDERER
Then 'tis he. The rest   10
That are within the note of expectation
Already are i' th' court.

FIRST MURDERER
      His horses go about.

15: **their walk:** at a walking pace (since the distance is nearly a mile, they probably have not dismounted to walk their horses); **A light, a light:** here is a light (the Second Murderer approaches Banquo under the pretense of answering Banquo's call for a light in line 9); **'Tis he:** that's him (the Third Murderer identifies Banquo in the light of his, the Third Murderer's, torch)

16: **Stand to't:** get ready

20: Scene: *Who did strike out the light:* During the scuffle with Banquo and Fleance, one, or all, of the torches are extinguished in some manner. One reading of this half-line would make it appear to be accidental, but another would make it the work of Third Murderer, albeit one with a puzzling motivation.

20: **Wast not the way:** wasn't that the plan

Costume rendering for the Murderers from the 1937 production at the Old Vic directed by Michel Saint-Denis

Rare Book and Special Collections Library, University of Illinois at Urbana-Champaign

THIRD MURDERER
  Almost a mile; but he does usually,
  So all men do, from hence to th' palace gate
  Make it their walk.
                          Enter BANQUO and FLEANCE with a torch

SECOND MURDERER
                      A light, a light!

THIRD MURDERER
                          'Tis he.   15

FIRST MURDERER
  Stand to't.

BANQUO
                      It will be rain tonight.

FIRST MURDERER
  Let it come down!

BANQUO
  O treachery! Fly, good Fleance, fly, fly, fly!

                                              [Exit FLEANCE]
  Thou mayst revenge. O slave!
                                              [BANQUO Dies]

THIRD MURDERER
  Who did strike out the light?

FIRST MURDERER
                      Wast not the way?   20

THIRD MURDERER
  There's but one down. The son is fled.

SECOND MURDERER
  We have lost best half of our affair.

FIRST MURDERER
  Well, let's away, and say how much is done.

                                              Exeunt

0: Scene: **Banquet prepared**: This scene at the Globe would have required the carrying onto the stage of a banquet table and the setting of it. Something similar is still the case today, though modern technology can often provide the prepared table without much effort. In the eighteenth and nineteenth centuries, the banquet was usually a very elaborate one with many glasses and other tableware and food and fruits piled high on the table (e.g., Macready's productions of the 1830s).

1: **degrees:** rank, for the order of seating

1–2: **first / And last:** all of you, no matter your rank

6: **state:** seat on the throne

7: **require:** request

9: Stage Direction: **Enter FIRST MURDERER:** In a number of productions, Nunn's for instance, the First Murderer's lines and actions are taken by Seyton/Servant.

10: **encounter thee:** return thanks for your welcome

11: **Both sides are even:** either thanks are mutual or there an equal number seated on both sides of the table

12: **large:** liberal; **measure:** toast

Act 3, Scene 4]

Banquet prepared. Enter MACBETH,
LADY [MACBETH], ROSS, LENNOX,
lords, and attendants.

MACBETH
You know your own degrees, sit down. At first
And last the hearty welcome.

Lords
Thanks to your majesty.

MACBETH
Ourself will mingle with society,
And play the humble host.   5
Our hostess keeps her state, but in best time
We will require her welcome.

LADY MACBETH
Pronounce it for me, sir, to all our friends,
For my heart speaks they are welcome.

Enter FIRST MURDERER

MACBETH
See, they encounter thee with their hearts' thanks.   10
Both sides are even. Here I'll sit i' th' midst.
Be large in mirth. Anon we'll drink a measure
The table round.

[Approaches FIRST MURDERER]
There's blood on thy face.

FIRST MURDERER
                        'Tis Banquo's then.

MACBETH
'Tis better thee without than he within.   15
Is he dispatched?

21: **perfect:** complete

22: **founded:** stable

23: **broad and general:** free and unconfined

24: **cabined, cribbed:** enclosed, shut in

25: **saucy:** insolent; **safe:** safely disposed of

28: **The least a death to nature:** i.e., the smallest of his gashes would have killed him

29: **worm:** young snake

32: **hear ourselves:** confer with each other

32–126: Scene: ***My royal . . . What is the night?:*** This scene can be played as one of utter chaos and confusion, but it is well to remember that there are actually four conversations, with or without lines, taking place in it. Macbeth, Lady Macbeth, and their guests, chiefly Lennox and Ross, are engaged in a public and formal one; Macbeth and Banquo's Ghost are engaged in another though the latter does not speak; Macbeth and Lady Macbeth are also engaged in a private one between themselves; and there is a kind of conversation carried on by the lords and attendants as they react to what they are seeing, not seeing, and hearing. An effort by the actors to keep these four kinds of address clear will not only provide the scene with the appropriate pace and structure but will no doubt assist in the movement of the actors on the stage. It is also worth noting that the scene almost winds down in exhaustion. When Macbeth asks, "What is the night?" and Lady Macbeth answers, "Almost at odds with morning, which is which," there is usually a feeling of tiredness and resignation on the parts of both of them.

33: **cheer:** toast; **sold:** not freely given, as in an inn where the host charges for the fare

34: **often vouched:** frequently affirmed, toasted

35: **To feed were best at home:** if all we needed to do was eat and drink we could do that at home

36: **From thence:** away from home; **sauce to meat is ceremony:** courteous conduct (ceremony) is what adds flavor (sauce) to the meat

FIRST MURDERER
                    My lord, his throat is cut.
      That I did for him.

MACBETH
                    Thou art the best o' th' cutthroats.
      Yet he's good that did the like for Fleance.
      If thou didst it, thou art the nonpareil.

FIRST MURDERER
      Most royal sir, Fleance is 'scaped.   20

MACBETH
      Then comes my fit again. I had else been perfect,
      Whole as the marble, founded as the rock,
      As broad and general as the casing air.
      But now I am cabined, cribbed, confined, bound in
      To saucy doubts and fears. But Banquo's safe?   25

FIRST MURDERER
      Ay, my good lord. Safe in a ditch he bides,
      With twenty trenched gashes on his head,
      The least a death to nature.

MACBETH
                    Thanks for that.
      There the grown serpent lies; the worm that's fled
      Hath nature that in time will venom breed,   30
      No teeth for the present. Get thee gone. Tomorrow
      We'll hear ourselves again.

                              Exit MURDERER

LADY MACBETH
                    My royal lord,
      You do not give the cheer. The feast is sold
      That is not often vouched, while 'tis a-making,
      'Tis given with welcome. To feed were best at home;   35
      From thence, the sauce to meat is ceremony;
      Meeting were bare without it.
              Enter the GHOST OF BANQUO, and sits in Macbeth's place

38: wait on: follow

40: our country's honor roofed: all the nobles under one roof

42–43: rather challenge for unkindness / Than pity for mischance: rather think he is absent through lack of manners than that he has had an accident

44: Lays blame upon his promise: shows a fault in manners (for not keeping his promise)

49: "Which of you have done this?": Christopher Walken as Macbeth and the Ensemble in the 1974 Public Theatre production directed by Edward Berkeley

Photo: George E. Joseph

MACBETH
                    Sweet remembrancer!
Now good digestion wait on appetite,
And health on both!

LENNOX
                    May't please your highness sit.

MACBETH
Here had we now our country's honor roofed,   40
Were the graced person of our Banquo present,
Who may I rather challenge for unkindness
Than pity for mischance.

ROSS
                    His absence, sir,
Lays blame upon his promise. Please't your highness
To grace us with your royal company.   45

MACBETH
The table's full.

LENNOX
                    Here is a place reserved, sir.

MACBETH
Where?

LENNOX
Here, my good lord. What is't that moves your highness?

MACBETH
Which of you have done this?

Lords
                    What, my good lord?

51: **gory locks:** bloody hair

Costume rendering for Banquo's Ghost from the 1937 production at the Old Vic directed by Michel Saint-Denis
Rare Book and Special Collections Library, University of Illinois at Urbana-Champaign

56: **note:** take note of

57: **passion:** disturbance

58: **Feed:** continue eating and drinking

61: **painting:** image or imagination

62: **air-drawn:** drawn in the air, or made of air

63: **flaws and starts:** outbursts

64: **Impostors:** impersonators; **well become:** be appropriate for

66: **Authorized:** on the authority of; **Shame itself:** for shame

71: **charnel houses:** crypts in churches or small buildings in churchyards for the bones of the dead

72: **monuments:** burial vaults

73: **maws:** stomachs; **kites:** birds of prey

MACBETH

    Thou canst not say I did it. *[To Banquo's Ghost]* Never shake   50
    Thy gory locks at me.

ROSS

    Gentlemen, rise. His highness is not well.

LADY MACBETH

    Sit, worthy friends. My lord is often thus,
    And hath been from his youth. Pray you, keep seat.
    The fit is momentary; upon a thought   55
    He will again be well. If much you note him
    You shall offend him and extend his passion.
    Feed, and regard him not.
                [To Macbeth] Are you a man?

MACBETH

    [To Lady Macbeth] Ay, and a bold one, that dare look on that
    Which might appall the devil.   60

LADY MACBETH

                [To Macbeth] O proper stuff!
    This is the very painting of your fear.
    This is the air-drawn dagger which you said
    Led you to Duncan. O, these flaws and starts,
    Impostors to true fear, would well become
    A woman's story at a winter's fire,   65
    Authorized by her grandam. Shame itself!
    Why do you make such faces? When all's done,
    You look but on a stool.

MACBETH

                [To Lady Macbeth] Prithee see there!
    Behold, look! *[To Banquo's Ghost]* Lo, how say you?
    Why, what care I, if thou canst nod, speak too?   70
    If charnel houses and our graves must send
    Those that we bury back, our monuments
    Shall be the maws of kites.

                    [Exit BANQUO'S GHOST]

76: **humane:** meaning both "humane" and "human"; **statute:** law; **purged the gentle weal:** made us civilized

78: **time:** "times" in the First Folio

81: **twenty mortal murders on their crowns:** see line 27: "twenty trenched gashes on his head"

84: **lack you:** miss your company

James Dale as Macbeth, Phyllis Neilson-Terry as Lady Macbeth, Guy Belmore as Banquo, and the Ensemble in the 1938 RSC production directed by B. Iden Payne
Ernest Daniels © Royal Shakespeare Company

LADY MACBETH

        [To Macbeth] What, quite unmanned in folly?

MACBETH

  [To Lady Macbeth] If I stand here, I saw him.

LADY MACBETH

        [To Macbeth] Fie, for shame!

MACBETH

  [To Lady Macbeth] Blood hath been shed ere now, i' th' olden time,   75
Ere humane statute purged the gentle weal;
Ay, and since too, murders have been performed
Too terrible for the ear. The [time] has been,
That when the brains were out the man would die,
And there an end. But now they rise again,   80
With twenty mortal murders on their crowns,
And push us from our stools. This is more strange
Than such a murder is.

LADY MACBETH

        My worthy lord,
Your noble friends do lack you.

MACBETH

        I do forget.
Do not muse at me, my most worthy friends.   85
I have a strange infirmity, which is nothing
To those that know me. Come, love and health to all,
Then I'll sit down. Give me some wine, fill full.

                    Enter [BANQUO'S] GHOST
I drink to the general joy o' th' whole table
And to our dear friend Banquo, whom we miss.   90
Would he were here! To all and him we thirst,
And all to all.

Lords

        Our duties, and the pledge.

93: "Avaunt, and quit my sight! Let the earth hide thee": Roger Allam as Macbeth and the Ensemble in the 1996 RSC production directed by Tim Albery

Photographer Reg Wilson © Royal Shakespeare Company

93: **Avaunt:** Go away; **quit:** leave

95: **speculation:** ability to see

97: **thing of custom:** normal occurrence

101: **armed rhinoceros:** so called because of the horn on its nose; **Hyrcan tiger:** Hyrcania was a region of the Roman Empire located to the southeast of the Caspian Sea; its tigers were legendary for their fierceness

104: **the desert:** an uninhabited place

105: **If trembling I inhabit:** if I continue to tremble

106: **baby of a girl:** female infant, or a baby girl's doll

107: **Unreal mock'ry:** illusion, perhaps with an added meaning of an illusion that mocks

110: **admired:** amazing

112–113: **strange / Even to the disposition that I owe:** a stranger to my own nature

MACBETH

[*To Banquo's Ghost*] Avaunt, and quit my sight! Let the earth hide thee.
Thy bones are marrowless, thy blood is cold;
Thou hast no speculation in those eyes   95
Which thou dost glare with.

LADY MACBETH

                           Think of this, good peers,
But as a thing of custom. 'Tis no other;
Only it spoils the pleasure of the time.

MACBETH

[*To Banquo's Ghost*] What man dare, I dare.
Approach thou like the rugged Russian bear   100
The armed rhinoceros, or th' Hyrcan tiger;
Take any shape but that, and my firm nerves
Shall never tremble. Or be alive again,
And dare me to the desert with thy sword.
If trembling I inhabit then, protest me   105
The baby of a girl. Hence, horrible shadow!
Unreal mock'ry, hence!

                                             [Exit BANQUO'S GHOST]
                           Why so, being gone,
I am a man again. [*To the others*] Pray you, sit still.

LADY MACBETH

You have displaced the mirth, broke the good meeting,
With most admired disorder.

MACBETH

                           Can such things be,   110
And overcome us like a summer's cloud,
Without our special wonder? You make me strange
Even to the disposition that I owe,
When now I think you can behold such sights,
And keep the natural ruby of your cheeks,   115
When mine is blanched with fear.

119: Stand not upon the order of your going: don't bother leaving by the order of your ranks

122: It will . . . will have blood: perhaps an allusion to Genesis 9:6, "Whoso sheddeth man's blood, by man shall his blood be shed."

122: "Blood will have blood": Jon Finch as Macbeth and Francesca Annis as Lady Macbeth in *The Tragedy of Macbeth* (1971) directed by Roman Polanski
Courtesy: Douglas Lanier

124: Augurs: divinations or predictions; **understood relations:** understandings of cause and effect

125: maggot pies: magpies; **choughs:** jackdaws or crows; pronounced "chuffs"; **brought forth:** revealed

126: What is the night: what time is it

128–129: denies his person / At our great bidding: refused our royal invitation

ROSS

> What sights, my lord?

LADY MACBETH

I pray you, speak not, he grows worse and worse.
Question enrages him. At once, good night.
Stand not upon the order of your going,
But go at once.

LENNOX

> Good night, and better health   120
Attend his majesty.

LADY MACBETH

> A kind good night to all.

> *Exeunt lords [and attendants]*

MACBETH

It will have blood, they say; blood will have blood.
Stones have been known to move and trees to speak;
Augurs and understood relations have
By maggot pies and choughs and rooks brought forth   125
The secret'st man of blood. What is the night?

LADY MACBETH

Almost at odds with morning, which is which.

MACBETH

How say'st thou, that Macduff denies his person
At our great bidding?

LADY MACBETH

> Did you send to him, sir?

130: **by the way:** secondhand; **send:** send for him

132: **servant fee'd:** paid informer or spy

133: **betimes:** early

137: **more:** further

139–140: **will to hand, / Which must be acted:** demand to be acted upon

140: **scanned:** carefully considered

141: **season:** seasoning

142: **self-abuse:** delusions

143: **initiate:** beginner's; **wants:** lacks; **hard use:** rigorous practice

MACBETH

    I hear it by the way, but I will send.   130
    There's not a one of them but in his house
    I keep a servant fee'd. I will tomorrow,
    And betimes I will, to the weird sisters.
    More shall they speak; for now I am bent to know,
    By the worst means, the worst. For mine own good,   135
    All causes shall give way. I am in blood
    Stepped in so far that, should I wade no more,
    Returning were as tedious as go o'er.
    Strange things I have in head, that will to hand,
    Which must be acted ere they may be scanned.   140

LADY MACBETH

    You lack the season of all natures, sleep.

MACBETH

    Come, we'll to sleep. My strange and self-abuse
    Is the initiate fear that wants hard use.
    We are yet but young in deed.

                                  Exeunt

0: Scene: It is now believed by most editors, scholars, and critics that this scene and some of the passages in 4.1 are not by Shakespeare but rather were added, directly or indirectly, by Thomas Middleton from his play, *The Witch*. Much of the argument revolves around the unusual role of Hecate and the use of rhyme. This scene is regularly cut, whether or not the director thinks it to be Shakespearean, as it does little to advance the action. Irving (1876 and 1888), Tree (1911), Nunn (1976), Bogdanov (1997), and Doran (1999) all did so. Frequently, the next scene is also cut so that the action progresses from the end of 3.4 to the opening of 4.1.

2: **beldams:** old women, or hags

3: **Saucy:** impudent

7: **close:** secret

8: **bear:** take

15: **Acheron:** one of the rivers of Hades in Greek mythology

18: **vessels:** cauldrons

21: **Unto:** working on

26: **sleights:** tricks or artifices

27: **artificial:** skilled in artifice and deceit

29: **confusion:** damnation

Act 3, Scene 5]

Thunder. Enter the three WITCHES, meeting HECATE.

FIRST WITCH
Why, how now, Hecate, you look angerly?

HECATE
Have I not reason, beldams as you are,
Saucy and overbold? How did you dare
To trade and traffic with Macbeth
In riddles and affairs of death,   5
And I, the mistress of your charms,
The close contriver of all harms,
Was never called to bear my part,
Or show the glory of our art?
And which is worse, all you have done   10
Hath been but for a wayward son,
Spiteful and wrathful, who, as others do,
Loves for his own ends, not for you.
But make amends now. Get you gone,
And at the pit of Acheron   15
Meet me i' th' morning; thither he
Will come to know his destiny.
Your vessels and your spells provide,
Your charms and every thing beside.
I am for th' air. This night I'll spend   20
Unto a dismal and a fatal end.
Great business must be wrought ere noon.
Upon the corner of the moon
There hangs a vaporous drop profound.
I'll catch it ere it come to ground,   25
And that distilled by magic sleights,
Shall raise such artificial sprites
As by the strength of their illusion
Shall draw him on to his confusion.
He shall spurn fate, scorn death, and bear   30

32: **security:** a false sense of safety

35: Stage Direction: ***Song:*** The song, "Come away," included in the First Folio, is from Middleton's *The Witch* (3.3) and begins, "Come away! Come away! / Hecate, Hecate, come away!"

Costume rendering for the First Witch from the 1937 production at the Old Vic directed by Michel Saint-Denis

Rare Book and Special Collections Library, University of Illinois at Urbana-Champaign

His hopes 'bove wisdom, grace, and fear.
And you all know, security
Is mortals' chiefest enemy.

Music and a song

Hark! I am called. My little spirit, see,
Sits in a foggy cloud, and stays for me.   35
Exit. Song within. "Come away, come away," etc.

FIRST WITCH
Come, let's make haste. She'll soon be back again.

Exeunt

0: Scene: All the major productions from Garrick in the 1740s through Beerbohm Tree at the beginning of the twentieth century cut this scene, as do Polanski and Doran. It is a scene like 2.4 (Ross and the Old Man) which comments, Chorus-like, on the events that have transpired and what they may mean.

1: **hit your thoughts:** agreed with what you already thought

2: **which can interpret further:** from which you can draw your own conclusions

3: **borne:** done

8: **want the thought:** fail to think

12: **delinquents:** criminals

13: **thralls:** slaves

18: **under his key:** imprisoned, locked up

19: **an't:** if it

21: **broad words:** blunt and open speech

22: **tyrant's:** the first time in the play this term is applied to Macbeth, and this by one present at the banquet of which he is speaking

24: **son:** Malcolm; "Sonnes" in the First Folio

25: **holds:** withholds; **due of birth:** the crown, his birthright

27: **pious Edward:** Edward the Confessor, king of England (1042–1066); noted for his piety and good rule, he was canonized in 1161 by Pope Alexander III

28–29: **nothing / Takes:** does not detract

29: **his high respect:** the respect due his rank as king

Act 3, Scene 6]

Enter LENNOX and another lord

LENNOX
    My former speeches have but hit your thoughts,
    Which can interpret further. Only I say
    Things have been strangely borne. The gracious Duncan
    Was pitied of Macbeth; marry, he was dead.
    And the right valiant Banquo walked too late. 5
    Whom you may say, if't please you, Fleance killed,
    For Fleance fled. Men must not walk too late.
    Who cannot want the thought how monstrous
    It was for Malcolm and for Donalbain
    To kill their gracious father? Damnèd fact, 10
    How it did grieve Macbeth! Did he not straight
    In pious rage the two delinquents tear
    That were the slaves of drink and thralls of sleep?
    Was not that nobly done? Ay, and wisely, too,
    For 'twould have angered any heart alive 15
    To hear the men deny't. So that I say
    He has borne all things well. And I do think
    That had he Duncan's sons under his key
    (As, an't please heaven, he shall not) they should find
    What 'twere to kill a father. So should Fleance. 20
    But, peace; for from broad words and 'cause he failed
    His presence at the tyrant's feast, I hear
    Macduff lives in disgrace. Sir, can you tell
    Where he bestows himself?

Lord
                The [son] of Duncan
    (From whom this tyrant holds the due of birth) 25
    Lives in the English court and is received
    Of the most pious Edward with such grace
    That the malevolence of fortune nothing
    Takes from his high respect. Thither Macduff

30: **aid:** support for Malcolm

31: **Northumberland:** English county bordering Scotland; **Siward:** family name of the Earls of Northumberland

33: **ratify:** sanction or approve

36: **free honors:** freely bestowed honors

38: **the:** "their" in the First Folio

41: **Sir, not I:** Macduff's answer to Macbeth's messenger

42: **cloudy:** gloomy; **turns me his back:** turns his back to me

43: **as who should say:** as if to say

44: **clogs:** burdens

45: **him:** Macduff

Is gone to pray the holy king, upon his aid   30
To wake Northumberland and warlike Siward
That, by the help of these (with Him above
To ratify the work) we may again
Give to our tables meat, sleep to our nights,
Free from our feasts and banquets bloody knives,   35
Do faithful homage and receive free honors,
All which we pine for now. And this report
Hath so exasperate [the] king that he
Prepares for some attempt of war.

LENNOX
    Sent he to Macduff?   40

Lord
    He did, and with an absolute "Sir, not I,"
The cloudy messenger turns me his back
And hums, as who should say "You'll rue the time
That clogs me with this answer."

LENNOX
              And that well might
Advise him to a caution t' hold what distance   45
His wisdom can provide. Some holy angel
Fly to the court of England and unfold
His message ere he come, that a swift blessing
May soon return to this our suffering country
Under a hand accursed.   50

Lord
    I'll send my prayers with him.

                                       Exeunt

[Macbeth

Act 4

1–38:
Orson Welles as Macbeth and the Three Witches

0: Scene: again imagined to be on a heath or other wild place

Preliminary sketch for the witches from the 1937 production at the Old Vic directed by Michel Saint-Denis
Rare Book and Special Collections Library, University of Illinois at Urbana-Champaign

1: **brinded:** brindled, striped

2: **hedge-pig:** hedgehog

3: **Harpier:** probably the Third Witch's familiar spirit

6–9: **Toad ... pot:** first boil the toad that has sweated venom under a stone for thirty-one days, or a full month

12: **fenny:** marsh or fen dweller

16: **fork:** tongue, **blindworm:** snake

17: **howlet:** owlet, small owl

Act 4, Scene 1]

FIRST WITCH
   Thrice the brinded cat hath mewed.

SECOND WITCH
   Thrice and once the hedge-pig whined.

THIRD WITCH
   Harpier cries "'Tis time, 'tis time!"

FIRST WITCH
   Round about the cauldron go.
   In the poisoned entrails throw.   5
   Toad, that under cold stone
   Days and nights has thirty-one
   Sweltered venom sleeping got,
   Boil thou first i' th' charmèd pot.

All
   Double, double toil and trouble,   10
   Fire burn, and cauldron bubble.

SECOND WITCH
   Fillet of a fenny snake,
   In the cauldron boil and bake.
   Eye of newt and toe of frog,
   Wool of bat and tongue of dog,   15
   Adder's fork and blindworm's sting,
   Lizard's leg and howlet's wing,
   For a charm of powerful trouble,
   Like a hell-broth boil and bubble.

All
   Double, double toil and trouble,   20
   Fire burn and cauldron bubble.

tracks30-31

1–38:
Orson Welles as Macbeth and the three witches

23: **mummy:** mummified flesh; **maw and gulf:** voracious devouring stomach

24: **ravined:** ravenous

27: **slips:** twigs

30: **birth-strangled:** strangled right after birth or during delivery (accidentally) by the umbilical cord

31: **drab:** whore

32: **slab:** thick, semi-liquid

33: **chaudron:** guts

43: Stage Direction: ***Music and a song: "Black Spirits," etc.*:** As with the song at the last appearance of Hecate (3.5), this is also taken from Middleton's *The Witch* and was obviously intended to be used in productions of *Macbeth* in Shakespeare's time.

THIRD WITCH
> Scale of dragon, tooth of wolf,
> Witches' mummy, maw and gulf
> Of the ravined salt-sea shark,
> Root of hemlock digged i' th' dark,   25
> Liver of blaspheming Jew,
> Gall of goat, and slips of yew
> Slivered in the moon's eclipse,
> Nose of Turk and Tartar's lips,
> Finger of birth-strangled babe   30
> Ditch-delivered by a drab,
> Make the gruel thick and slab.
> Add thereto a tiger's chaudron,
> For the ingredients of our cauldron.

All
> Double, double toil and trouble,   35
> Fire burn and cauldron bubble.

SECOND WITCH
> Cool it with a baboon's blood,
> Then the charm is firm and good.
>> *Enter HECATE [to] the other three WITCHES*

HECATE
> O, well done! I commend your pains,
> And every one shall share i' th' gains.   40
> And now about the cauldron sing,
> Like elves and fairies in a ring,
> Enchanting all that you put in.
>> *Music and a song: "Black Spirits," etc.*
>> *[Exit HECATE]*

SECOND WITCH
> By the pricking of my thumbs,
> Something wicked this way comes.   45
> Open, locks,
> Whoever knocks!

>> *Enter MACBETH*

53: **yeasty:** foamy or frothing

54: **Confound:** destroy; **navigation:** shipping

55: **bladed corn:** unripe grain; **lodged:** beaten down by wind and rain

56: **warders':** guards or watch, related to "warden"

58–59: **the treasure / Of nature's germens:** the seeds from which all existence springs; the First Folio reads "Germaine"

60: **destruction sicken:** destruction itself becomes sick from its own overindulgence

Sir Derek Jacobi as Macbeth with Virginia Denham, Tracy-Ann Oberman, and Marjorie Yates as the witches in the 1993 RSC production directed by Adrian Noble
Photo: Donald Cooper

MACBETH

How now, you secret, black, and midnight hags?
What is't you do?

All

A deed without a name.

MACBETH

I conjure you, by that which you profess   50
(Howe'er you come to know it), answer me.
Though you untie the winds and let them fight
Against the churches, though the yeasty waves
Confound and swallow navigation up,
Though bladed corn be lodged and trees blown down,   55
Though castles topple on their warders' heads,
Though palaces and pyramids do slope
Their heads to their foundations, though the treasure
Of nature's [germens] tumble all together,
Even till destruction sicken, answer me   60
To what I ask you.

FIRST WITCH

Speak.

SECOND WITCH

Demand.

THIRD WITCH

We'll answer.

FIRST WITCH

Say, if th' hadst rather hear it from our mouths
Or from our masters'.

MACBETH

Call 'em. Let me see 'em.

65: **farrow:** litter of pigs; **sweaten:** sweated

66: **gibbet:** gallows

68: **Thyself and office:** your appearance and your message

68: Stage Direction: ***Armed Head:*** head enclosed in helmet of a suit of armor.

68: Scene: Here, and at lines 76 and 86, it is quite clear that the apparitions appear and speak lines although the direction "enter" is not used. On Shakespeare's stage there is no reason for them to be anything other than a representation of what they are said to be, carried in on a pole by an actor who then speaks their lines. However, unlike Banquo's Ghost, it appears that there is no choice about whether they are present. After 1660 it became possible to have the apparitions appear in ever greater detail and elaboration, though recently this trend has reversed. Nunn has the witches show Macbeth emblems like shrunken heads on sticks while they speak the apparitions' lines. In Doran's production, the apparitions were tortured faces showing through a membrane on the back wall of the stage.

71: "Macbeth! Macbeth! Macbeth! Beware Macduff!": Patrick Page as Macbeth with Jewel Robinson, Sarah Marshall, and Naomi Jacobson as the witches in the Shakespeare Theatre Company's 2004–05 production directed by Michael Kahn
Photo: Richard Termine

74: **harped:** sounded or stated

FIRST WITCH
Pour in sow's blood, that hath eaten
Her nine farrow; grease that's sweaten   65
From the murderer's gibbet throw
Into the flame.

All
                Come, high or low;
Thyself and office deftly show.
         Thunder. First Apparition: an Armed Head.

MACBETH
Tell me, thou unknown power—

FIRST WITCH
             He knows thy thought.
Hear his speech, but say thou naught.   70

FIRST APPARITION
Macbeth! Macbeth! Macbeth! Beware Macduff!
Beware the thane of Fife! Dismiss me. Enough.
                  He descends

MACBETH
Whate'er thou art, for thy good caution, thanks.
Thou hast harped my fear aright. But one word more,—

FIRST WITCH
He will not be commanded. Here's another   75
More potent than the first.
        Thunder. Second Apparition: a Bloody Child.

SECOND APPARITION
Macbeth! Macbeth! Macbeth!—

MACBETH
Had I three ears, I'd hear thee.

84: **bond of fate:** a guarantee or contract with fate (that killing Macduff will make the Second Apparition's "assurances" to be "double sure")

87: **issue of a king:** heir to the throne

88–89: **the round / And top of sovereignty:** the crown

91: **Be lion-mettled:** have the spirit of a lion

92: **chafes:** is irritated

96: **impress:** compel, conscript, or draft into service

97: **his:** its; **bodements:** prophecies

98: **Rebellious dead:** may be a reference to Banquo, but perhaps Macbeth is thinking of all those killed so far and soon to be killed to get and keep the throne, hence "rebellious"

100: **live the lease of nature:** live out his natural life

101: **mortal custom:** usual or normal time of death

Jack Carter as Macbeth and the Ensemble in the 1936 production at the New Lafayette Theatre directed by Orson Welles

Library of Congress, Music Division, Federal Theatre Project Collection

SECOND APPARITION
> Be bloody, bold, and resolute. Laugh to scorn
> The power of man, for none of woman born   80
> Shall harm Macbeth.

> *[He] Descends*

MACBETH
> Then live, Macduff; what need I fear of thee?
> But yet I'll make assurance double sure
> And take a bond of fate. Thou shalt not live,
> That I may tell pale-hearted fear it lies,   85
> And sleep in spite of thunder.

> *Thunder. Third Apparition:*
> *a Child Crowned, with a tree in his hand.*
>   What is this
> That rises like the issue of a king
> And wears upon his baby-brow the round
> And top of sovereignty?

All
> Listen, but speak not to't.   90

THIRD APPARITION
> Be lion-mettled, proud, and take no care
> Who chafes, who frets, or where conspirers are.
> Macbeth shall never vanquished be until
> Great Birnam Wood to high Dunsinane Hill
> Shall come against him.

> *[He] descends*

MACBETH
>   That will never be.   95
> Who can impress the forest, bid the tree
> Unfix his earth-bound root? Sweet bodements, good!
> Rebellious dead, rise never till the wood
> Of Birnam rise, and our high-placed Macbeth
> Shall live the lease of nature, pay his breath   100
> To time and mortal custom. Yet my heart
> Throbs to know one thing. Tell me, if your art
> Can tell so much: shall Banquo's issue ever
> Reign in this kingdom?

Costume rendering for a king apparition from the 1937 production at the Old Vic directed by Michel Saint-Denis

Rare Book and Special Collections Library, University of Illinois at Urbana-Champaign

112: Stage Direction: F1, "*A shew of eight Kings, and Banquo last, with a glasse in his hand.*" From what follows, this appears to mean that the eighth king has a looking glass in his hand and that Banquo, or the Ghost of Banquo, the ninth member of the procession, leads them on. The Stage Direction has been emended to make this clear. The use of the word "show" in this direction fairly clearly indicates that what went on at the Globe was a dumb show of eight actors dressed in royal fashion and crowned and led onto the stage by Banquo's Ghost. In the eighteenth and nineteenth centuries this procession was often carried out behind a transparent backscene or in silhouette. Nunn has the witches blindfold Macbeth and leave him alone so that the procession is entirely in Macbeth's mind and of his imaginings. Doran has Macbeth see only the Ghost of Banquo and a vision of Fleance and substantially cuts the speech after line 114.

115: other: second

117: Start: burst forth

118: crack of doom: judgment day, the "crack" may be a reference to thunder or to the splitting of the firmament on Doomsday

122: twofold balls and treble scepters: the basic reference is to the orb and scepter used in the coronation ceremony; "twofold" probably means England and Scotland; "treble" is almost certainly a reference to the title James assumed in 1604 of "King of Great Britain, France, and Ireland"

All
> Seek to know no more.

MACBETH
> I will be satisfied. Deny me this,   105
> And an eternal curse fall on you! Let me know!

> *[Cauldron sinks]*

> Why sinks that cauldron?

> *Hautboys*

> And what noise is this?

FIRST WITCH
> Show!

SECOND WITCH
> Show!

THIRD WITCH
> Show!   110

All
> Show his eyes, and grieve his heart.
> Come like shadows; so depart.
> *A show of eight kings, the last with a glass in his hand,*
> *[following the GHOST OF BANQUO]*

MACBETH
> Thou art too like the spirit of Banquo. Down!
> Thy crown does sear mine eyeballs. And thy hair,
> Thou other gold-bound brow, is like the first.   115
> A third is like the former. Filthy hags,
> Why do you show me this? A fourth! Start, eyes!
> What, will the line stretch out to the crack of doom?
> Another yet! A seventh! I'll see no more.
> And yet the eighth appears, who bears a glass   120
> Which shows me many more, and some I see
> That twofold balls and treble scepters carry.
> Horrible sight! Now I see 'tis true,

124: **the blood-boltered Banquo:** Banquo, whose hair is matted with blood

126–133: it is assumed that these lines and the music that follows were added by some other author; unlike the other instances in this play, it is impossible to guess what this music might have been

127: **amazedly:** as in a trance

128: **sprites:** spirits

131: **antic round:** fantastical or outlandish dance

135: **aye:** always; **in the calendar:** perhaps Macbeth is thinking of the church calendar, though the court or governmental calendar are also possibilities

136: **without there:** you who are outside

For the blood-boltered Banquo smiles upon me,
And points at them for his.

[Apparitions vanish]

           What, is this so?   125

FIRST WITCH
    Ay, sir, all this is so. But why
    Stands Macbeth thus amazedly?
    Come, sisters, cheer we up his sprites,
    And show the best of our delights.
    I'll charm the air to give a sound,   130
    While you perform your antic round.
    That this great king may kindly say,
    Our duties did his welcome pay.

Music. The witches dance and vanish.

MACBETH
    Where are they? Gone? Let this pernicious hour
    Stand aye accursed in the calendar!—   135
    Come in, without there!

Enter LENNOX

LENNOX
           What's your grace's will?

MACBETH
    Saw you the weird sisters?

LENNOX
           No, my lord.

MACBETH
    Came they not by you?

LENNOX
           No, indeed, my lord.

142–143: "'Tis two or three, my lord, that bring you word / Macduff is fled to England": Andrew Laurence as Lennox in *The Tragedy of Macbeth* (1971) directed by Roman Polanski

Courtesy: Douglas Lanier

145: **anticipat'st:** forestalls or prevents

146–147: **flighty purpose never is o'ertook / Unless the deed go with it:** fleeting ("flighty") purposes are never accomplished unless action is taken to bring them about

148: **firstlings:** firstborn (the sense here and in the next line is that his first thoughts must be followed by his first acts)

151: **surprise:** attack suddenly

154: **trace him in his line:** descend from him

156: **sights:** visions or hallucinations

MACBETH
   Infected be the air whereon they ride.
   And damned all those that trust them! I did hear   140
   The galloping of horse. Who was't came by?

LENNOX
   'Tis two or three, my lord, that bring you word
   Macduff is fled to England.

MACBETH
             Fled to England!

LENNOX
   Ay, my good lord.

MACBETH [*aside*]
   Time, thou anticipat'st my dread exploits.   145
   The flighty purpose never is o'ertook
   Unless the deed go with it. From this moment
   The very firstlings of my heart shall be
   The firstlings of my hand. And even now,
   To crown my thoughts with acts, be it thought and done: 150
   The castle of Macduff I will surprise.
   Seize upon Fife, give to th' edge o' th' sword
   His wife, his babes, and all unfortunate souls
   That trace him in his line. No boasting like a fool;
   This deed I'll do before this purpose cool.   155
   But no more sights!—
             [*To LENNOX*] Where are these gentlemen?
   Come, bring me where they are.

                                               Exeunt

0: Location: Macduff's castle in Fife

0: Scene: The scene needs have nothing more than the three actors named. Although nothing in the lines says who the woman and child are, Macbeth's lines at the end of the previous scene ("The castle of Macduff I will surprise. / Seize upon Fife, give to th' edge o' th' sword / His wife, his babes, and all unfortunate souls / That trace him in his line.") clearly identify them. Modern productions have attempted to domesticate the scene by having Lady Macduff bathing her son (as in Polanski's and Doran's) or performing other domestic duties with her children.

Costume rendering for Lady Macduff from the 1937 production at the Old Vic directed by Michel Saint-Denis

Rare Book and Special Collections Library, University of Illinois at Urbana-Champaign

9: **wants the natural touch:** lacks the natural feelings of a father and husband

14: **coz:** cousin or kinswoman

15: **school:** teach or control

17: **fits o' th' season:** the temper of the times

18–22: **But cruel . . . move:** times are bad when we may be held to be traitors for reasons we neither know nor understand

Act 4, Scene 2]

LADY MACDUFF
  What had he done, to make him fly the land?

ROSS
  You must have patience, madam.

LADY MACDUFF
                    He had none.
  His flight was madness. When our actions do not,
  Our fears do make us traitors.

ROSS
                    You know not
  Whether it was his wisdom or his fear.   5

LADY MACDUFF
  Wisdom? To leave his wife, to leave his babes,
  His mansion and his titles in a place
  From whence himself does fly? He loves us not;
  He wants the natural touch; for the poor wren
  (The most diminutive of birds) will fight,   10
  Her young ones in her nest, against the owl.
  All is the fear and nothing is the love,
  As little is the wisdom, where the flight
  So runs against all reason.

ROSS
                    My dearest coz,
  I pray you, school yourself. But for your husband,   15
  He is noble, wise, judicious, and best knows
  The fits o' th' season. I dare not speak much further;
  But cruel are the times when we are traitors
  And do not know ourselves when we hold rumor

23: **Shall:** it shall

25–26: **My pretty . . . you:** this is addressed to Macduff's son

29: **It would be . . . your discomfort:** I would weep and disgrace myself and upset you

33: **As birds do, mother:** reference to Matthew 6:26: "Behold the fowls of the air; for they sow not, neither do they reap . . . yet your heavenly Father feedeth them."

35: **Poor bird:** a bird of no use as game and therefore not worth catching

35–36: **net . . . lime . . . pitfall . . . gin:** methods of catching birds, the net, pitfall, and gin are various kinds of snares; lime is birdlime, a sticky substance

Costume rendering for the Son of Macduff from the 1937 production at the Old Vic directed by Michel Saint-Denis

Rare Book and Special Collections Library, University of Illinois at Urbana-Champaign

From what we fear, yet know not what we fear,   20
But float upon a wild and violent sea
Each way and move. I take my leave of you.
Shall not be long but I'll be here again.
Things at the worst will cease, or else climb upward
To what they were before. My pretty cousin,   25
Blessing upon you.

LADY MACDUFF
　Fathered he is, and yet he's fatherless.

ROSS
　I am so much a fool, should I stay longer,
　It would be my disgrace and your discomfort.
　I take my leave at once.   30
                                                                Exit

LADY MACDUFF
　Sirrah, your father's dead.
　And what will you do now? How will you live?

SON
　As birds do, mother.

LADY MACDUFF
　　　　　　　　What, with worms and flies?

SON
　With what I get, I mean; and so do they.

LADY MACDUFF
　Poor bird, thou'dst never fear the net nor lime,   35
　The pitfall nor the gin.

SON
　Why should I, mother? Poor birds they are not set for.
　My father is not dead, for all your saying.

43–44: "Thou speak'st with all thy wit; and yet, i' faith, / With wit enough for thee": Melissa T. Miller as Lady Macduff and Peter Vance as Young Macduff in The Shakespeare Theatre of New Jersey's 2004 production directed by Bonnie J. Monte

Photo: Gerry Goodstein

43: **wit:** intelligence

44: **wit enough for thee:** intelligence, or wit, enough for your age

48: **swears and lies:** swearing an oath of loyalty and then being false in loyalty is the way Lady Macduff appears to define treason, while her son takes it as a more general definition of swearing and lying

ACT 4 : SCENE 2   [LINES 39–52

LADY MACDUFF
Yes, he is dead. How wilt thou do for a father?

SON
Nay, how will you do for a husband?   40

LADY MACDUFF
Why, I can buy me twenty at any market.

SON
Then you'll buy 'em to sell again.

LADY MACDUFF
Thou speak'st with all thy wit; and yet, i' faith,
With wit enough for thee.

SON
Was my father a traitor, mother?   45

LADY MACDUFF
Ay, that he was.

SON
What is a traitor?

LADY MACDUFF
Why, one that swears and lies.

SON
And be all traitors that do so?

LADY MACDUFF
Every one that does so is a traitor, and must be hanged.   50

SON
And must they all be hanged that swear and lie?

LADY MACDUFF
Every one.

61–62: I am not . . . perfect: you do not know me but I know your position and reputation

63: doubt: suspect or fear

64: homely: ordinary or common

65: "Be not found here. Hence with your little ones": Michelle Shupe as Lady Macduff and the Ensemble in the Shakespeare Theatre Company's 2004–05 production directed by Michael Kahn
Photo: Richard Termine

67: fell: fatal

68: too nigh your person: (the danger is) too near you

73: Accounted: judged

SON
  Who must hang them?

LADY MACDUFF
  Why, the honest men.

SON
  Then the liars and swearers are fools, for there are liars and   55
  swearers enough to beat the honest men and hang up them.

LADY MACDUFF
  Now, God help thee, poor monkey! But how wilt thou do for a father?

SON
  If he were dead, you'd weep for him. If you would not, it were a
  good sign that I should quickly have a new father.

LADY MACDUFF
  Poor prattler, how thou talk'st!   60

                                                  Enter a messenger

Messenger
  Bless you, fair dame. I am not to you known,
  Though in your state of honor I am perfect.
  I doubt some danger does approach you nearly.
  If you will take a homely man's advice,
  Be not found here. Hence with your little ones.   65
  To fright you thus, methinks, I am too savage;
  To do worse to you were fell cruelty,
  Which is too nigh your person. Heaven preserve you!
  I dare abide no longer.

                                                           Exit

LADY MACDUFF
                    Whither should I fly?
  I have done no harm. But I remember now   70
  I am in this earthly world, where to do harm
  Is often laudable, to do good sometime
  Accounted dangerous folly. Why then, alas,

75–81: Scene: Davenant and Garrick cut these lines and they were not restored to productions of the play until Phelps's production of 1847. As with the killing of Banquo in 3.3, one of the Murderers has often been Seyton/Servant.

79: **shag-haired:** unkempt or uncouth

79–80: **egg . . . fry:** the young of birds and of fish respectively

Do I put up that womanly defense,
To say I have done no harm?

Enter MURDERERS

              What are these faces?   75

FIRST MURDERER
Where is your husband?

LADY MACDUFF
I hope, in no place so unsanctified
Where such as thou mayst find him.

FIRST MURDERER
              He's a traitor.

SON
Thou liest, thou shag-haired villain!

FIRST MURDERER
              What, you egg?

[Stabbing him]

Young fry of treachery!

SON
              He has killed me, mother.   80
Run away, I pray you.

[Dies]
Exit [LADY MACDUFF], crying "Murder!"
[Exeunt MURDERERS, following her, carrying SON'S body]

0: Location: England, at the Court of King Edward the Confessor (1003–1066)

0: Scene: Most directors from Garrick forward have made substantial cuts in this scene, the longest (243 lines) in the play, particularly in the long opening exchange between Malcolm and Macduff (lines 1 to 139).

1: **desolate:** solitary, lonely, or deserted

3: **mortal sword:** sword that brings death

4: **Bestride:** stand astride, as when protecting a fallen comrade in battle; **downfall'n:** "downfall" in the First Folio; **birthdom:** land of our birth, by analogy with "kingdom"

6: **that:** so that

8: **Like syllable:** similar to the sound; **dolor:** anguish

10: **time to friend:** opportunity

12: **sole:** only or mere

13: **honest:** honorable

15: **deserve:** "discerne" in the First Folio; **deserve of him through me:** try to gain something from Macbeth by betraying me (as the following image of the sacrificial lamb image makes more plain); **wisdom:** it may be thought wise

19–20: **A good and virtuous . . . imperial charge:** a royal demand might make even the honorable give in

21: **transpose:** change your basic character

Act 4, Scene 3]

MALCOLM
Let us seek out some desolate shade, and there
Weep our sad bosoms empty.

MACDUFF
           Let us rather
Hold fast the mortal sword, and like good men,
Bestride our [downfall'n] birthdom. Each new morn
New widows howl, new orphans cry, new sorrows   5
Strike heaven on the face, that it resounds
As if it felt with Scotland and yelled out
Like syllable of dolor.

MALCOLM
           What I believe I'll wail;
What know, believe; and what I can redress,
As I shall find the time to friend, I will.   10
What you have spoke, it may be so, perchance.
This tyrant, whose sole name blisters our tongues,
Was once thought honest. You have loved him well.
He hath not touched you yet. I am young, but something
You may [deserve] of him through me, and wisdom   15
To offer up a weak poor innocent lamb
T' appease an angry god.

MACDUFF
I am not treacherous.

MALCOLM
           But Macbeth is.
A good and virtuous nature may recoil
In an imperial charge. But I shall crave your pardon.   20
That which you are my thoughts cannot transpose.

23–24: **all things . . . look so:** foul things would try to look fair (graced) but even so, fair things will still be fair

25: **even there:** in that very place

26: **rawness:** exposed or cruel place

27: **motives:** reasons or inducements

29: **jealousies:** suspicions; **dishonors:** dishonor you

30: **mine own safeties:** my suspiciousness protects me; **rightly just:** truly honorable

32: **basis sure:** secure foundations

33: **Wear thou thy wrongs:** (the country should) wear the wrongs it has suffered as a badge or heraldic device

34: **The title:** Macbeth's title to the kingdom; **affeered:** confirmed

36: **whole space:** the entire kingdom of Scotland

37: **rich East:** the Orient, fabled for wealth in Shakespeare's time

38: **absolute:** complete

43: **England:** Edward the Confessor, King of England

44: **goodly thousands:** many thousands of good troops

46: **wear it on my sword:** carry Macbeth's severed head on the point of his sword

48: **More suffer:** shall suffer more

49: **succeed:** succeed to the throne

Angels are bright still, though the brightest fell;
Though all things foul would wear the brows of grace,
Yet grace must still look so.

MACDUFF
                    I have lost my hopes.

MALCOLM
Perchance even there where I did find my doubts.   25
Why in that rawness left you wife and child,
Those precious motives, those strong knots of love,
Without leave-taking? I pray you,
Let not my jealousies be your dishonors,
But mine own safeties. You may be rightly just,   30
Whatever I shall think.

MACDUFF
                    Bleed, bleed, poor country!
Great tyranny, lay thou thy basis sure,
For goodness dare not check thee. Wear thou thy wrongs;
The title is affeered. Fare thee well, lord.
I would not be the villain that thou think'st   35
For the whole space that's in the tyrant's grasp,
And the rich East to boot.

MALCOLM
                    Be not offended.
I speak not as in absolute fear of you.
I think our country sinks beneath the yoke.
It weeps, it bleeds, and each new day a gash   40
Is added to her wounds. I think withal
There would be hands uplifted in my right;
And here from gracious England have I offer
Of goodly thousands. But, for all this,
When I shall tread upon the tyrant's head,   45
Or wear it on my sword, yet my poor country
Shall have more vices than it had before,
More suffer and more sundry ways than ever,
By him that shall succeed.

51: **particulars:** various types; **grafted:** engrafted, as in grafting trees and shrubs

52: **opened:** displayed

55: **confineless:** without bounds, unconfined

58: **Luxurious:** lecherous

59: **Sudden:** peremptory and violent

61: **voluptuousness:** addiction to sensual pleasure

63: **cistern:** here used to mean "pit" or perhaps "cesspit"

64: **continent:** chaste or restraints of chastity

65: **will:** desires

70–72: **You may . . . hoodwink:** you may satisfy your pleasures in secret and still have a seemingly cold image

73–76: **There cannot . . . inclined:** you cannot be so ravenous (vulture-like) that you will take more women than will willingly give themselves to you because you are king

Robert Taber as Macduff from the 1898 production at the Lyceum Theatre
Mary Evans Picture Library

MACDUFF
                    What should he be?

MALCOLM
    It is myself I mean, in whom I know   50
    All the particulars of vice so grafted
    That, when they shall be opened, black Macbeth
    Will seem as pure as snow, and the poor state
    Esteem him as a lamb, being compared
    With my confineless harms.

MACDUFF
                    Not in the legions   55
    Of horrid hell can come a devil more damned
    In evils to top Macbeth.

MALCOLM
                    I grant him bloody,
    Luxurious, avaricious, false, deceitful,
    Sudden, malicious, smacking of every sin
    That has a name. But there's no bottom, none,   60
    In my voluptuousness. Your wives, your daughters,
    Your matrons and your maids, could not fill up
    The cistern of my lust, and my desire
    All continent impediments would o'erbear
    That did oppose my will. Better Macbeth   65
    Than such a one to reign.

MACDUFF
                    Boundless intemperance
    In nature is a tyranny. It hath been
    The untimely emptying of the happy throne
    And fall of many kings. But fear not yet
    To take upon you what is yours. You may   70
    Convey your pleasures in a spacious plenty,
    And yet seem cold, the time you may so hoodwink.
    We have willing dames enough. There cannot be
    That vulture in you, to devour so many
    As will to greatness dedicate themselves,   75
    Finding it so inclined.

77: **ill-composed affection:** evil disposition

78: **stanchless:** insatiable

80: **his jewels:** one noble's jewels

82: **forge:** create, perhaps with some sense of "forgery"

85: **Sticks deeper:** concerns the whole kingdom

86: **summer-seeming:** apparently youthful

87: **sword:** reason for the death

88: **foisons:** large supplies

89: **your mere own:** your own royal property by itself; **portable:** supportable

92: **As:** such as

93: **lowliness:** humility

95: **have no relish:** do not relish

96: **division:** the parts or features of

99: **confound:** destroy

MALCOLM
                    With this there grows
In my most ill-composed affection such
A stanchless avarice that, were I king,
I should cut off the nobles for their lands,
Desire his jewels and this other's house.   80
And my more-having would be as a sauce
To make me hunger more, that I should forge
Quarrels unjust against the good and loyal,
Destroying them for wealth.

MACDUFF
                    This avarice
Sticks deeper, grows with more pernicious root   85
Than summer-seeming lust, and it hath been
The sword of our slain kings. Yet do not fear.
Scotland hath foisons to fill up your will.
Of your mere own. All these are portable,
With other graces weighed.   90

MALCOLM
But I have none. The king-becoming graces,
As justice, verity, temperance, stableness,
Bounty, perseverance, mercy, lowliness,
Devotion, patience, courage, fortitude,
I have no relish of them, but abound   95
In the division of each several crime,
Acting it many ways. Nay, had I power, I should
Pour the sweet milk of concord into hell,
Uproar the universal peace, confound
All unity on earth.

MACDUFF
                    O Scotland, Scotland!   100

MALCOLM
If such a one be fit to govern, speak.
I am as I have spoken.

104: **untitled:** usurping

106: **truest issue:** right and lawful heir to the throne

107: **interdiction:** accusation

108: **blaspheme his breed:** curses his own family line

111: **Died every day she lived:** died to the world every day of her life by mortification of her flesh

114: **passion:** show of emotions

118: **trains:** plans or wiles

119: **modest wisdom:** wise prudence; **plucks:** prevents, pulls me back

123: **abjure:** recant, solemnly reject

125: **For:** as

126: **Unknown to woman:** i.e., a virgin; **was forsworn:** broke an oath

131: **upon:** about

133: **thy here-approach:** "they heere approach" in the First Folio

135: **at a point:** fully armed and ready

137: **warranted quarrel:** justification to act

MACDUFF
                    Fit to govern?
No, not to live. O nation miserable,
With an untitled tyrant bloody-sceptered,
When shalt thou see thy wholesome days again,   105
Since that the truest issue of thy throne
By his own interdiction stands accursed,
And does blaspheme his breed? Thy royal father
Was a most sainted king. The queen that bore thee,
Oft'ner upon her knees than on her feet,   110
Died every day she lived. Fare thee well.
These evils thou repeat'st upon thyself
Have banished me from Scotland. O my breast,
Thy hope ends here!

MALCOLM
                    Macduff, this noble passion,
Child of integrity, hath from my soul   115
Wiped the black scruples, reconciled my thoughts
To thy good truth and honor. Devilish Macbeth
By many of these trains hath sought to win me
Into his power, and modest wisdom plucks me
From overcredulous haste. But God above   120
Deal between thee and me, for even now
I put myself to thy direction, and
Unspeak mine own detraction, here abjure
The taints and blames I laid upon myself,
For strangers to my nature. I am yet   125
Unknown to woman, never was forsworn,
Scarcely have coveted what was mine own,
At no time broke my faith, would not betray
The devil to his fellow, and delight
No less in truth than life. My first false speaking   130
Was this upon myself. What I am truly
Is thine and my poor country's to command.
Whither indeed, before thy here-approach,
Old Siward, with ten thousand warlike men,
Already at a point, was setting forth.   135
Now we'll together, and the chance of goodness
Be like our warranted quarrel. Why are you silent?

140: **forth:** out of his private chambers

142: **stay:** wait for; **convinces:** defeats, confounds

143: **assay:** test or trial; **art:** medicine

145: **presently:** immediately

146–156: **'Tis called the evil . . . healing benediction:** Scrofula, popularly known as "the king's evil," is a chronic enlargement and degeneration of the lymphatic glands. It was supposed that the touch of a king or queen could cure, or improve, the condition. In England this custom is believed to have started with Edward the Confessor but the earliest records of touching for the king's evil are in the reign of Edward III, when, after the ritual ablutions of the sufferers, they were touched by the king with an angel coin (so called because it had a stamped image of St. Michael on it), which was then given to them as a talisman. The touching reached its peak of popularity in the reign of Charles II. William III (William of Orange) refused to touch and referred applicants to James II in exile in France. Anne revived the practice but when she died in 1714, the succeeding Hanoverian monarchs (George I-William IV) refused to continue the practice and it died out.

150: **strangely visited people:** those afflicted with this strange disease

152: **mere:** total

153: **Hanging a golden stamp:** after Edward touches the diseased, a golden medal, stamped with a particular image, is hung about their necks

156: **virtue:** power or ability

MACDUFF
  Such welcome and unwelcome things at once
  'Tis hard to reconcile.

                                                    Enter a doctor

MALCOLM
  Well, more anon.—Comes the king forth, I pray you?   140

Doctor
  Ay, sir. There are a crew of wretched souls
  That stay his cure. Their malady convinces
  The great assay of art; but at his touch,
  Such sanctity hath heaven given his hand,
  They presently amend.

MALCOLM
                    I thank you, doctor.   145
                                                    Exit doctor

MACDUFF
  What's the disease he means?

MALCOLM
                    'Tis called the evil.
  A most miraculous work in this good king,
  Which often, since my here-remain in England,
  I have seen him do. How he solicits heaven,
  Himself best knows, but strangely visited people,   150
  All swoll'n and ulcerous, pitiful to the eye,
  The mere despair of surgery, he cures,
  Hanging a golden stamp about their necks,
  Put on with holy prayers; and, 'tis spoken,
  To the succeeding royalty he leaves   155
  The healing benediction. With this strange virtue,
  He hath a heavenly gift of prophecy,
  And sundry blessings hang about his throne,
  That speak him full of grace.

                                                    Enter ROSS

160: **not:** "nor" in the First Folio

162: **betimes:** early or soon

167: **But:** except

168: **rend:** tear

169: **Are made, not marked:** (these sounds) are made but no one remarks on them because they are so common

170–171: **The dead man's knell ... for who:** hardly anyone asks for whom the funeral bell is being rung (probably because it was so common)

173: **or ere:** before

174: **too nice:** too particular or too detailed

177: **teems:** brings forth in abundance

Arthur Bourchier as Macduff
Mary Evans Picture Library

MACDUFF

        See who comes here?

MALCOLM

  My countryman, but yet I know him [not].   160

MACDUFF

  My ever-gentle cousin, welcome hither.

MALCOLM

  I know him now. Good God, betimes remove
  The means that makes us strangers!

ROSS

        Sir, amen.

MACDUFF

  Stands Scotland where it did?

ROSS

        Alas, poor country,
  Almost afraid to know itself. It cannot   165
  Be called our mother, but our grave, where nothing
  But who knows nothing, is once seen to smile;
  Where sighs and groans and shrieks that rend the air
  Are made, not marked; where violent sorrow seems
  A modern ecstasy. The dead man's knell   170
  Is there scarce asked for who, and good men's lives
  Expire before the flowers in their caps,
  Dying or ere they sicken.

MACDUFF

  O, relation too nice, and yet too true!

MALCOLM

  What's the newest grief?   175

ROSS

  That of an hour's age doth hiss the speaker.
  Each minute teems a new one.

181: **niggard:** miser

184: **out:** out in the field; in arms

185–186: **Which was . . . afoot:** the rumor was confirmed by my seeing the king's army in the field against the rebels

187: **of:** for; **Your eye:** your presence

189: **doff:** put off or remove

Costume rendering for Ross from the 1937 production at the Old Vic directed by Michel Saint-Denis
Rare Book and Special Collections Library, University of Illinois at Urbana-Champaign

MACDUFF
                How does my wife?

ROSS
  Why, well.

MACDUFF
                And all my children?

ROSS
                        Well too.

MACDUFF
  The tyrant has not battered at their peace?

ROSS
  No, they were well at peace when I did leave 'em.   180

MACDUFF
  Be not a niggard of your speech. How goes't?

ROSS
  When I came hither to transport the tidings,
  Which I have heavily borne, there ran a rumor
  Of many worthy fellows that were out;
  Which was to my belief witnessed the rather   185
  For that I saw the tyrant's power afoot.
  Now is the time of help. Your eye in Scotland
  Would create soldiers, make our women fight,
  To doff their dire distresses.

MALCOLM
                Be't their comfort
  We are coming thither. Gracious England hath   190
  Lent us good Siward and ten thousand men;
  An older and a better soldier none
  That Christendom gives out.

Ian McDiarmid as Ross, Roger Rees as Malcolm, and Bob Peck as Macduff
in the 1978 RSC production directed by Trevor Nunn
Photo: Donald Cooper

195: **would:** should

196: **latch:** hear or catch

197: **fee-grief:** similar to the legal term "fee-simple," an estate belonging to only
one man and his heirs forever

198: **Due:** belonging

205: **surprised:** taken by surprise attack

207: **quarry:** pile

209: **pull your hat upon your brows:** typical practice to indicate mourning

210–211: **The grief . . . break:** to speak about one's grief can ease one's grief

211: **o'erfraught:** overburdened

ROSS

               Would I could answer
This comfort with the like. But I have words
That would be howled out in the desert air,   195
Where hearing should not latch them.

MACDUFF

              What concern they?
The general cause, or is it a fee-grief
Due to some single breast?

ROSS

              No mind that's honest
But in it shares some woe, though the main part
Pertains to you alone.

MACDUFF

              If it be mine,   200
Keep it not from me, quickly let me have it.

ROSS

Let not your ears despise my tongue forever,
Which shall possess them with the heaviest sound
That ever yet they heard.

MACDUFF

              Hum! I guess at it.

ROSS

Your castle is surprised, your wife and babes   205
Savagely slaughtered. To relate the manner
Were on the quarry of these murdered deer,
To add the death of you.

MALCOLM

             Merciful heaven!
What, man, ne'er pull your hat upon your brows.
Give sorrow words. The grief that does not speak   210
Whispers the o'erfraught heart and bids it break.

214: **from thence:** away from there (home)

219: **He:** It is usually assumed that Macduff is here referring to Macbeth but it is possible that he means Malcolm

219: "All my pretty ones?": John Stride as Ross, Terence Bayler as Macduff, and Stephen Chase as Malcolm in *The Tragedy of Macbeth* (1971) directed by Roman Polanski
Courtesy: Douglas Lanier

220: **hell-kite:** metaphorically, a bird of prey from Hell

221: **dam:** female parent

223: **Dispute:** think about

228: **Naught that I am:** sinful as I am

MACDUFF
  My children too?

ROSS
  Wife, children, servants, all that could be found.

MACDUFF
  And I must be from thence? My wife killed too?

ROSS
  I have said.   215

MALCOLM
  Be comforted.
  Let's make us med'cines of our great revenge
  To cure this deadly grief.

MACDUFF
  He has no children. All my pretty ones?
  Did you say all? O hell-kite! All?   220
  What, all my pretty chickens and their dam
  At one fell swoop?

MALCOLM
  Dispute it like a man.

MACDUFF
                  I shall do so,
  But I must also feel it as a man.
  I cannot but remember such things were   225
  That were most precious to me. Did heaven look on
  And would not take their part? Sinful Macduff,
  They were all struck for thee! Naught that I am,
  Not for their own demerits, but for mine,
  Fell slaughter on their souls. Heaven rest them now.   230

MALCOLM
  Be this the whetstone of your sword. Let grief
  Convert to anger. Blunt not the heart, enrage it.

233: **play the woman with mine eyes:** weep

235: **intermission:** delay; **Front to front:** face to face

238: **tune:** disposition, temper; "time" in the First Folio

239: **king:** Edward the Confessor

239: "Come, go we to the king": Brandon Demery as Malcolm, Andrew Long as Macduff, and Richard Pelzman as Ross in the Shakespeare Theatre Company's 2004–05 production directed by Michael Kahn
Photo: Richard Termine

240: **lack:** need; **leave:** permission to leave the royal court

242: **instruments:** armor and/or weapons

243: **The night . . . the day:** it is a long night that has no dawn (metaphoric)

MACDUFF
    O, I could play the woman with mine eyes
    And braggart with my tongue! But, gentle heavens,
    Cut short all intermission. Front to front   235
    Bring thou this fiend of Scotland and myself.
    Within my sword's length set him. If he 'scape,
    Heaven forgive him too.

MALCOLM
              This [tune] goes manly.
    Come, go we to the king. Our power is ready;
    Our lack is nothing but our leave. Macbeth   240
    Is ripe for shaking, and the powers above
    Put on their instruments. Receive what cheer you may.
    The night is long that never finds the day.

                                        Exeunt

[Macbeth

Act 5

0: Location: must take place somewhere in Macbeth's castle at Dunsinane; in the modern theater this scene is usually set either in Lady Macbeth's bedroom or in an anteroom near it

0: Stage Direction: **Physic**: medicine

1: **watched:** remained awake

2: **walked:** walked in her sleep

4: **nightgown:** dressing gown; **closet:** cabinet

8: **do the effects of watching:** act as if awake

12: **meet:** proper

13: Stage Direction: Lady Macbeth has traditionally entered carrying the candle indicated and in some form of nightdress or similar clothing. Famously, Francesca Annis, in Polanski's film, played this scene without any clothing at all.

14: **very guise:** usual way

14–15: "Lo you, here she comes ... stand close": Vivien Leigh as Lady Macbeth in the 1955 RSC production directed by Glen Byam Shaw

Act 5, Scene 1]

Enter a doctor of Physic and a waiting-gentlewoman

Doctor

I have two nights watched with you, but can perceive no truth in your
report. When was it she last walked?

Gentlewoman

Since his majesty went into the field, I have seen her rise from her
bed, throw her nightgown upon her, unlock her closet, take forth
paper, fold it, write upon't, read it, afterwards seal it, and again   5
return to bed; yet all this while in a most fast sleep.

Doctor

A great perturbation in nature, to receive at once the benefit of
sleep, and do the effects of watching. In this slumbery agitation,
besides her walking and other actual performances, what, at any
time, have you heard her say?   10

Gentlewoman

That, sir, which I will not report after her.

Doctor

You may to me, and 'tis most meet you should.

Gentlewoman

Neither to you nor any one, having no witness to confirm my speech.
                              Enter LADY [MACBETH] with a taper
Lo you, here she comes. This is her very guise and, upon my life,
fast asleep. Observe her, stand close.   15

Doctor

How came she by that light?

Gentlewoman

Why, it stood by her. She has light by her continually. 'Tis her
command.

21: "Look, how she rubs her hands": Kelly McGillis as Lady Macbeth, Emery Battis as the doctor, and Naomi Jacobson as Lady Macbeth's attendant in the Shakespeare Theatre Company's 2004–05 production directed by Michael Kahn

Photo: Richard Termine

22: **accustomed:** customary or usual

29–30: **call our power to / account:** make us answer for our conduct

35: **mar all:** ruin everything; **starting:** sudden fits

Doctor
You see, her eyes are open.

Gentlewoman
Ay, but their sense is shut.   20

Doctor
What is it she does now? Look, how she rubs her hands.

Gentlewoman
It is an accustomed action with her, to seem thus washing her
hands. I have known her continue in this a quarter of an hour.

LADY MACBETH
Yet here's a spot.

Doctor
Hark, she speaks. I will set down what comes from her, to satisfy my   25
remembrance the more strongly.

LADY MACBETH
Out, damned spot, out, I say! One. Two. Why then, 'tis time to
do't. Hell is murky. Fie, my lord, fie, a soldier and afeard? What
need we fear who knows it, when none can call our power to
account? Yet who would have thought the old man to have had so   30
much blood in him?

Doctor
Do you mark that?

LADY MACBETH
The thane of Fife had a wife. Where is she now? What, will these
hands ne'er be clean? No more o' that, my lord, no more o' that.
You mar all with this starting.   35

Doctor
Go to, go to, you have known what you should not.

tracks 32-34

24–54:
Pamela Brown as Lady Macbeth
Fiona Shaw as Lady Macbeth

39–40: "Here's the smell of the blood still. All the perfumes of Arabia will / not sweeten this little hand": Laila Robins as Lady Macbeth in The Shakespeare Theatre of New Jersey's 2004 production directed by Bonnie J. Monte
Photo: Gerry Goodstein

42: **sorely:** grievously; **charged:** burdened

47: **practice:** experience, though the doctor may mean his branch or knowledge of medicine

50: **on's:** of his

Gentlewoman
She has spoke what she should not, I am sure of that. Heaven
knows what she has known.

LADY MACBETH
Here's the smell of the blood still. All the perfumes of Arabia will
not sweeten this little hand.   40
O, O, O!

Doctor
What a sigh is there! The heart is sorely charged.

Gentlewoman
I would not have such a heart in my bosom for the dignity of the
whole body.

Doctor
Well, well, well.   45

Gentlewoman
Pray God it be, sir.

Doctor
This disease is beyond my practice. Yet I have known those which
have walked in their sleep who have died holily in their beds.

LADY MACBETH
Wash your hands, put on your nightgown. Look not so pale. I tell
you yet again, Banquo's buried; he cannot come out on's grave.   50

Doctor
Even so?

LADY MACBETH
To bed, to bed. There's knocking at the gate. Come, come, come,
come, give me your hand. What's done cannot be undone. To bed,
to bed, to bed.

Exit

55: "Will she go now to bed?": Judith Anderson as Lady Macbeth in the 1960 production directed by George Schaefer

Courtesy: Douglas Lanier

56: **Directly:** at once

62: **annoyance:** injury, in this case, self-injury

64: **mated:** checkmated, or puzzled

Doctor
    Will she go now to bed?   55

Gentlewoman
    Directly.

Doctor
    Foul whisp'rings are abroad. Unnatural deeds
    Do breed unnatural troubles. Infected minds
    To their deaf pillows will discharge their secrets.
    More needs she the divine than the physician.   60
    God, God forgive us all. Look after her.
    Remove from her the means of all annoyance,
    And still keep eyes upon her. So, good night.
    My mind she has mated, and amazed my sight.
    I think, but dare not speak.

Gentlewoman
                Good night, good doctor.   65
                                                  Exeunt

0: Location: the countryside, around the castle of Dunsinane

0: Scene: Almost all major productions from Davenant until the early twentieth century cut the entire scene; Nunn cut lines 2 through the first half of 11 and 26–31.

4: **grim:** threatening

5: **Excite:** awake or quicken; **mortified man:** dead man

8: **file:** list

10: **unrough:** smooth (not yet shaving)

11: **Protest:** assert; **first of manhood:** entry into the manly art of war

15: **distempered:** diseased; in this usage, swollen with disease

Act 5, Scene 2]

*Drum and colors. Enter MENTEITH, CAITHNESS,
ANGUS, LENNOX, [and] soldiers.*

MENTEITH
The English power is near, led on by Malcolm,
His uncle Siward and the good Macduff.
Revenges burn in them, for their dear causes
Would to the bleeding and the grim alarm
Excite the mortified man.

ANGUS
                Near Birnam Wood   5
Shall we well meet them. That way are they coming.

CAITHNESS
Who knows if Donalbain be with his brother?

LENNOX
For certain, sir, he is not. I have a file
Of all the gentry. There is Siward's son,
And many unrough youths that even now   10
Protest their first of manhood.

MENTEITH
                What does the tyrant?

CAITHNESS
Great Dunsinane he strongly fortifies.
Some say he's mad; others that lesser hate him
Do call it valiant fury. But for certain,
He cannot buckle his distempered cause   15
Within the belt of rule.

18: **minutely:** every minute; **upbraid:** censure; **faith-breach:** disloyalty, the breaking of his oath of loyalty to Duncan

23: **pestered:** annoyed with constant troubles; **recoil and start:** leap back with a start

27: **weal:** state or commonwealth

28–29: **pour . . . us:** we will pour the last drops of our blood as a purgative for the ills of the kingdom

Soldiers in the 1936 production at the New Lafayette Theatre directed by Orson Welles
Library of Congress, Music Division, Federal Theatre Project Collection

ANGUS
                    Now does he feel
His secret murders sticking on his hands.
Now minutely revolts upbraid his faith-breach.
Those he commands move only in command,
Nothing in love. Now does he feel his title   20
Hang loose about him, like a giant's robe
Upon a dwarfish thief.

MENTEITH
                    Who, then, shall blame
His pestered senses to recoil and start,
When all that is within him does condemn
Itself for being there?

CAITHNESS
                    Well, march we on   25
To give obedience where 'tis truly owed.
Meet we the med'cine of the sickly weal,
And with him pour we in our country's purge
Each drop of us.

LENNOX
                    Or so much as it needs,
To dew the sovereign flower and drown the weeds.   30
Make we our march towards Birnam.

                                        Exeunt marching

0: Location: usually set in a room in the castle of Dunsinane

3: **taint:** be seized or infected

5: **All mortal consequences:** all the things that can happen to mankind

8: **epicures:** those given to luxury and gluttony; perhaps a Scottish taunt of the better table manners of the English

9: **sway:** rule

11: **cream-faced:** white, pale; **loon:** fool

12: **goose look:** foolish, timid look

16: **prick thy face, and over-red thy fear:** pinch, or prick, your cheeks to make the paleness of your fear appear to be the redness of bravery

17: **patch:** fool, or yokel

18: **of thy:** on thy; **linen:** white, pale

19: **whey-face:** pale-faced

Act 5, Scene 3]

MACBETH
Bring me no more reports. Let them fly all.
Till Birnam Wood remove to Dunsinane,
I cannot taint with fear. What's the boy Malcolm?
Was he not born of woman? The spirits that know
All mortal consequences have pronounced me thus: 5
"Fear not, Macbeth. No man that's born of woman
Shall e'er have power upon thee." Then fly, false thanes,
And mingle with the English epicures.
The mind I sway by and the heart I bear
Shall never sag with doubt nor shake with fear.   10

Enter [a] servant

The devil damn thee black, thou cream-faced loon!
Where got'st thou that goose look?

Servant
There is ten thousand—

MACBETH
Geese, villain?

Servant
Soldiers, sir.   15

MACBETH
Go prick thy face, and over-red thy fear,
Thou lily-livered boy. What soldiers, patch?
Death of thy soul! Those linen cheeks of thine
Are counselors to fear. What soldiers, whey-face?

Servant
The English force, so please you.   20

22: **push:** action or effort

23: **disseat:** dethrone or unseat; "dis-eate" in the First Folio

25: **sere:** withered or dried

27: **As:** such as

29: **mouth-honor:** lip service

30: **fain:** wish to, or gladly

36: **Skirr:** scour, or search

38: **sick:** physically ill

39: **thick-coming:** frequently occurring; **fancies:** hallucinations or fantastic thoughts

Costume rendering for the doctor from the 1937 production at the Old Vic directed by Michel Saint-Denis
Rare Book and Special Collections Library, University of Illinois at Urbana-Champaign

MACBETH
Take thy face hence.

[Exit servant]

     Seyton!—I am sick at heart,
When I behold—Seyton, I say!—This push
Will cheer me ever, or [disseat] me now.
I have lived long enough. My way of life
Is fall'n into the sere, the yellow leaf,   25
And that which should accompany old age,
As honor, love, obedience, troops of friends,
I must not look to have, but in their stead
Curses, not loud but deep, mouth-honor, breath,
Which the poor heart would fain deny, and dare not. Seyton!   30

Enter SEYTON

SEYTON
What is your gracious pleasure?

MACBETH
     What news more?

SEYTON
All is confirmed, my lord, which was reported.

MACBETH
I'll fight till from my bones my flesh be hacked.
Give me my armor.

SEYTON
     'Tis not needed yet.

MACBETH
I'll put it on.   35
Send out more horses. Skirr the country round.
Hang those that talk of fear. Give me mine armor.
How does your patient, Doctor?

Doctor
     Not so sick, my lord,
As she is troubled with thick-coming fancies,
That keep her from her rest.

42: **rooted:** planted deeply

43: **Raze out:** remove

44: **oblivious:** sleep inducing, or causing oblivion

48: **physic:** medicine

50: **send out:** perhaps the phrase was to be "send out orders" but in the confusion Macbeth does not finish it

51: **dispatch:** hurry

51–52: **cast ... disease:** analyze the urine (water) as a method of diagnoses

53: **purge:** rid the body of unhealthy matter (laxatives are purges)

56: **rhubarb:** used as a purgative; **senna:** cassia, and related medicinal plants, producing cathartic and emetic effects; the First Folio reads "Cyme," which is probably an error for the older spelling of senna, "cynne"

57: **scour:** to evacuate the stomach and/or bowels through purging

60: **death and bane:** death in battle or death by murder (bane)

MACBETH
                    Cure her of that.   40
    Canst thou not minister to a mind diseased,
    Pluck from the memory a rooted sorrow,
    Raze out the written troubles of the brain,
    And with some sweet oblivious antidote
    Cleanse the stuffed bosom of that perilous stuff   45
    Which weighs upon the heart?

Doctor
                    Therein the patient
    Must minister to himself.

MACBETH
    Throw physic to the dogs. I'll none of it.—
    Come, put mine armor on. Give me my staff.
    Seyton, send out.—Doctor, the thanes fly from me.—   50
    Come, sir, dispatch.—If thou couldst, doctor, cast
    The water of my land, find her disease,
    And purge it to a sound and pristine health,
    I would applaud thee to the very echo,
    That should applaud again.—Pull't off, I say.—   55
    What rhubarb, senna, or what purgative drug
    Would scour these English hence? Hear'st thou of them?

Doctor
    Ay, my good lord. Your royal preparation
    Makes us hear something.

MACBETH
                    Bring it after me.
    I will not be afraid of death and bane,   60
    Till Birnam forest come to Dunsinane.

Doctor
    [Aside] Were I from Dunsinane away and clear,
    Profit again should hardly draw me here.

                                                        Exeunt

0: Location: logically located in or near Birnam Wood

0: Scene: Although often substantially cut, this is an important scene if some effort is going to be made to represent the moving Birnam Wood. The stage direction at 5.6 has the army entering "with boughs."

2: **chambers:** rooms in our houses

5: **shadow:** hide

6: **host:** army; **discovery:** military intelligence

8: **We learn no other but:** our intelligence tells us that

Costume rendering for Mentieth and Caithness from the 1937 production at the Old Vic directed by Michel Saint-Denis
Rare Book and Special Collections Library, University of Illinois at Urbana-Champaign

10: **setting down before't:** laying siege to it

Act 5, Scene 4]

*Drum and colors. Enter MALCOLM, SIWARD and
[YOUNG] SIWARD, MACDUFF, MENTEITH,
CAITHNESS, ANGUS, LENNOX, ROSS,
and soldiers, marching.*

MALCOLM
    Cousins, I hope the days are near at hand
    That chambers will be safe.

MENTEITH
                We doubt it nothing.

SIWARD
    What wood is this before us?

MENTEITH
                The wood of Birnam.

MALCOLM
    Let every soldier hew him down a bough
    And bear't before him. Thereby shall we shadow   5
    The numbers of our host and make discovery
    Err in report of us.

Soldiers
                It shall be done.

SIWARD
    We learn no other but the confident tyrant
    Keeps still in Dunsinane, and will endure
    Our setting down before't.

11: **there is advantage to be given:** opportunity presents itself

12: **more and less:** nobles and commoners; **given . . . revolt:** revolted from him

14–15: **Let our just censures / Attend the true event:** let us make no judgments until we have won. Siward repeats this thought in different words in the following speech.

19: "Thoughts speculative their unsure hopes relate": Alf Joint as Siward in *The Tragedy of Macbeth* (1971) directed by Roman Polanski
Courtesy: Douglas Lanier

MALCOLM
                    'Tis his main hope;   10
    For where there is advantage to be given,
    Both more and less have given him the revolt,
    And none serve with him but constrainèd things
    Whose hearts are absent too.

MACDUFF
                    Let our just censures
    Attend the true event, and put we on   15
    Industrious soldiership.

SIWARD
                    The time approaches
    That will with due decision make us know
    What we shall say we have and what we owe.
    Thoughts speculative their unsure hopes relate,
    But certain issue strokes must arbitrate;   20
    Towards which advance the war.

                                        Exeunt, marching

0: Location: As Macbeth's opening lines make clear, this scene is set on the battlements of Dunsinane Castle. Although some would like to set this scene outside the castle, there is a practical problem: the cry of women at line 7 needs to be heard, and it is improbable that it could be heard from a distance. Most modern productions set this scene either on the battlements or in the hall.

4: **ague:** violent fever

5: **forced:** reinforced; **those . . . ours:** deserters from Macbeth's forces

6: **dareful:** defiantly

7: Stage Directions: ***A cry within of women:*** In the First Folio the cry is clearly thought to be that of Lady Macbeth's women attendants. However, those who wish to make actual Malcolm's speculation at 5.7.99–101 ("his fiend-like queen, / Who, as 'tis thought, by self and violent hands / Took off her life.") have often had the cry be that of one woman, Lady Macbeth.

10: **cooled:** been chilled

11: **my fell of hair:** the hair on my head; "fell" means a covering of hair, particularly a thick and matted one

12: **treatise:** tale

13: **As:** as if

14: **Direness:** dreadfulness

Act 5, Scene 5]

Enter MACBETH, SEYTON, and soldiers,
with drum and colors

MACBETH
    Hang out our banners on the outward walls.
    The cry is still "They come!" Our castle's strength
    Will laugh a siege to scorn. Here let them lie
    Till famine and the ague eat them up.
    Were they not forced with those that should be ours,   5
    We might have met them dareful, beard to beard,
    And beat them backward home.

A cry within of women

             What is that noise?

SEYTON
    It is the cry of women, my good lord.

[Exit]

MACBETH
    I have almost forgot the taste of fears
    The time has been, my senses would have cooled   10
    To hear a night-shriek, and my fell of hair
    Would at a dismal treatise rouse and stir
    As life were in't. I have supped full with horrors.
    Direness, familiar to my slaughterous thoughts
    Cannot once start me.

[Re-enter SEYTON]

             Wherefore was that cry?   15

SEYTON
    The queen, my lord, is dead.

tracks 35-37

17–28:
Orson Welles as Macbeth
Stephen Dillane as Macbeth

17: **hereafter:** at a later time, or perhaps in another place

18: **word:** the word, we presume, is death

19–21: "Tomorrow, and tomorrow, and tomorrow . . . of recorded time": Patrick Page as Macbeth in the Shakespeare Theatre Company's 2004–05 production directed by Michael Kahn
Photo: Richard Termine

20: **petty:** slow

21: **last syllable of recorded time:** end of recorded history

24: **player:** actor

34: **anon:** all at once

MACBETH
    She should have died hereafter;
    There would have been a time for such a word.
    Tomorrow, and tomorrow, and tomorrow,
    Creeps in this petty pace from day to day   20
    To the last syllable of recorded time,
    And all our yesterdays have lighted fools
    The way to dusty death. Out, out, brief candle,
    Life's but a walking shadow, a poor player
    That struts and frets his hour upon the stage   25
    And then is heard no more. It is a tale
    Told by an idiot, full of sound and fury,
    Signifying nothing.

Enter a messenger

    Thou comest to use thy tongue; thy story quickly.

Messenger
    Gracious my lord,   30
    I should report that which I say I saw,
    But know not how to do it.

MACBETH
              Well, say, sir.

Messenger
    As I did stand my watch upon the hill,
    I looked toward Birnam, and anon, methought,
    The wood began to move.

MACBETH
              Liar and slave!   35

Messenger
    Let me endure your wrath, if't be not so.
    Within this three mile may you see it coming.
    I say, a moving grove.

40: **cling:** shrivel; **sooth:** true

42: **pull in:** take hold of; **resolution:** determination

47: **avouches:** asserts

50: **estate o' th' world:** the whole world, or at least Macbeth's existence on it; **undone:** destroyed

51: **wrack:** disaster

52: **harness:** armor

Godfery Tearle as Macbeth in the 1949 RSC production directed by Anthony Quayle
Mary Evans Picture Library

MACBETH

               If thou speak'st false,
Upon the next tree shalt thou hang alive,
Till famine cling thee. If thy speech be sooth,   40
I care not if thou dost for me as much.
I pull in resolution, and begin
To doubt the equivocation of the fiend
That lies like truth. "Fear not till Birnam Wood
Do come to Dunsinane," and now a wood   45
Comes toward Dunsinane.—Arm, arm, and out!—
If this which he avouches does appear,
There is nor flying hence nor tarrying here.
I 'gin to be aweary of the sun,
And wish the estate o' th' world were now undone.—   50
Ring the alarum-bell! Blow, wind! Come, wrack,
At least we'll die with harness on our back.

                                              Exeunt

0: **Location:** just before the castle of Dunsinane

0: **Scene:** This scene and this entry, which must only exist to display the moving Birnam Wood, have the potential for creating travesty and humor. The branches the actors carry before them, if that is indeed what they do, must be significant enough to make an impact of the vision of the audience. One of the most successful stagings was Doran's production at the Swan Theatre in Stratford. The boughs were tall enough and wide enough to completely fill the opening at the back of the stage so that a moving wood did seem to be advancing toward the audience. Too often actors are forced to carry things that look like reject Christmas trees or else stylized versions of branches, which do not have quite the same effect. We do not know what was done at the Globe but it was not significant enough for our one witness to have mentioned it.

The army arrives at Dunsinane in the 1960 production directed by George Schaefer
Courtesy: Douglas Lanier

4: **battle:** contingent, or battalion

6: **order:** plan of battle

7: **power:** army

8: **fight:** win the fight

10: **harbingers:** foretellers or forerunners

Act 5, Scene 6]

Drum and colors. Enter MALCOLM, SIWARD,
MACDUFF, and their army, with boughs.

MALCOLM
    Now near enough. Your leafy screens throw down
    And show like those you are. You, worthy uncle,
    Shall, with my cousin, your right-noble son,
    Lead our first battle. Worthy Macduff and we
    Shall take upon's what else remains to do,   5
    According to our order.

SIWARD
                Fare you well.
    Do we but find the tyrant's power tonight,
    Let us be beaten, if we cannot fight.

MACDUFF
    Make all our trumpets speak; give them all breath,
    Those clamorous harbingers of blood and death.   10
                                  Exeunt

0: Location: Conventionally editors have located this scene in "another part of the field," but there is no reason against, and several reasons for, locating it within the castle of Dunsinane.

0: Scene: This scene begins immediately outside the castle; after the action at line 63, it moves to just inside the castle (see Siward's "Enter, sir, the castle" at line 29). The first sixty lines of this scene form a circular motion of combatants entering, fighting (or looking for someone to fight), exiting, entering again, fighting, and the victorious carrying off the slain. That the action is continuous is indicated by the repeated accompaniment of the exits and entrances by alarums (lines 13, 23, 29, 37, and 63).

1–2: **stake . . . bear-like:** Macbeth invokes the image of bear baiting, where the bear was tied to a stake in the center of the arena and then dogs were set upon it

8: **title:** name

11: Scene: *[They] fight*: Here, and at lines 37 and 63, the mere direction "fight" covers a multitude of actions. Some recent productions have treated all fights as unarmed combat of a martial arts sort. In Ayliff's 1928 modern dress production, Macbeth first empties his revolver into Macduff who, because of his "charmèd life," is not wounded. Others have had only a few sword thrusts, while those with expertise in stage combat have staged rather elaborate fights. In Shakespeare's era, when many men carried weapons as a matter of course, such combat would have had to be realistic; today it is usually much more like choreography.

Patrick Page as Macbeth and Kip Pierson as Young Siward in the Shakespeare Theatre Company's 2004–05 production directed by Michael Kahn

Photo: Richard Termine

Act 5, Scene 7]

Enter MACBETH

MACBETH
  They have tied me to a stake. I cannot fly,
  But, bear-like, I must fight the course. What's he
  That was not born of woman? Such a one
  Am I to fear, or none.

Enter YOUNG SIWARD

YOUNG SIWARD
  What is thy name?

MACBETH
                Thou'lt be afraid to hear it.   5

YOUNG SIWARD
  No, though thou call'st thyself a hotter name
  Than any is in hell.

MACBETH
                My name's Macbeth.

YOUNG SIWARD
  The devil himself could not pronounce a title
  More hateful to mine ear.

MACBETH
                No, nor more fearful.

YOUNG SIWARD
  Thou liest, abhorrèd tyrant. With my sword   10
  I'll prove the lie thou speak'st.

[They] fight, and Young Siward [is] slain

13: Stage Direction: **with Young Siward's body**: Since neither Macduff nor Malcolm and Siward notices Young Siward's body when they enter, it must be the case that the Stage Direction in the First Folio ("*Exit*") is incomplete and Macbeth must, as the only live actor on stage at this point, carry the body off.

17: **kerns:** Irish mercenary foot soldiers

18: **staves:** weapons; **Either thou, Macbeth:** either I find you, Macbeth

20: **undeeded:** unused

21: **clatter:** noise

22: **bruited:** reported, shouted for or at

24: **gently rendered:** surrendered without opposition

25–26: **The tyrant's . . . war:** a number of Macbeth's people now fight on our side and the nobles fight well for us

27: **The day . . . yours:** you have nearly won

29: **strike beside us:** fight on our side

MACBETH

        Thou wast born of woman,
But swords I smile at, weapons laugh to scorn,
Brandished by man that's of a woman born.

              Exit [with YOUNG SIWARD's body]
              Alarums. Enter MACDUFF.

MACDUFF

That way the noise is. Tyrant, show thy face!
If thou be'st slain and with no stroke of mine,   15
My wife and children's ghosts will haunt me still.
I cannot strike at wretched kerns, whose arms
Are hired to bear their staves. Either thou, Macbeth,
Or else my sword with an unbattered edge
I sheathe again undeeded. There thou shouldst be;   20
By this great clatter, one of greatest note
Seems bruited. Let me find him, fortune,
And more I beg not.

                    Exit
        Alarums. Enter MALCOLM and SIWARD.

SIWARD

This way, my lord. The castle's gently rendered.
The tyrant's people on both sides do fight,   25
The noble thanes do bravely in the war.
The day almost itself professes yours,
And little is to do.

MALCOLM

          We have met with foes
That strike beside us.

SIWARD

         Enter, sir, the castle.

                Exeunt
       Alarum. Enter MACBETH.

30-63:
Hugh Ross as Macbeth and Gary Bakewell as Macduff
Orson Welles as Macbeth and George Coulouris as Macduff

30: **Roman fool:** refers to the practice of Roman commanders committing suicide; Shakespeare had previously portrayed this in *Julius Caesar* and *Antony and Cleopatra*
32: Scene: *Turn, hellhound, turn!:* Macduff's half line indicates that Macbeth must be in the process of exiting again to fight Malcolm's troops when Macduff sees him.
34: **charged:** filled, or loaded

Jack Carter as Macbeth and Maurice Ellis as Macduff in the 1936 production at the New Lafayette Theatre, directed by Orson Welles
Library of Congress, Music Division, Federal Theatre Project Collection

37: **terms:** words; **give thee out:** describe you; **Thou losest labor:** you waste your effort
38: **intrenchant:** incapable of being cut
39: **impress:** mark, or stamp
40: **crests:** helmets
43: **angel:** devil, fallen angel
44-45: **from . . . Untimely ripped:** the assumption is that Macduff was delivered by cesarean section, which, it appears, does not count as being "of woman born" since it is not natural childbirth; **Untimely:** prematurely
47: **cowed:** intimidated; **better part of man:** manhood, or courage
48: **juggling:** tricky or deceitful
49: **palter:** equivocate or prevaricate; **double sense:** ambiguously, with a double meaning

MACBETH
  Why should I play the Roman fool, and die   30
  On mine own sword? Whiles I see lives, the gashes
  Do better upon them.

                     Enter MACDUFF

MACDUFF
          Turn, hellhound, turn!

MACBETH
  Of all men else I have avoided thee.
  But get thee back. My soul is too much charged
  With blood of thine already.

MACDUFF
          I have no words;   35
  My voice is in my sword. Thou bloodier villain
  Than terms can give thee out.

                     Fight. Alarum.

MACBETH
          Thou losest labor.
  As easy mayst thou the intrenchant air
  With thy keen sword impress as make me bleed.
  Let fall thy blade on vulnerable crests;   40
  I bear a charmèd life, which must not yield,
  To one of woman born.

MACDUFF
          Despair thy charm,
  And let the angel whom thou still hast served
  Tell thee, Macduff was from his mother's womb
  Untimely ripped.   45

MACBETH
  Accursèd be that tongue that tells me so,
  For it hath cowed my better part of man!
  And be these juggling fiends no more believed,
  That palter with us in a double sense,
  That keep the word of promise to our ear,   50
  And break it to our hope. I'll not fight with thee.

30–63:
Hugh Ross as Macbeth and Gary Bakewell as Macduff
Orson Welles as Macbeth and George Coulouris as Macduff

53: **gaze:** spectacle

55: **Painted on a pole:** his painted picture mounted on a pole, like a shop sign; **underwrit:** with a legend or description written below the picture

58: **baited:** challenged, or attacked (the image is that of bear or bull baiting)

60: **opposed:** as my opponent

61: **try:** test, or attempt

63: Stage Direction: ***Macduff exits carrying Macbeth's body:*** The removal of Macbeth's body is not solely for the reason mentioned at line 13 but also to enable Malcolm and his troops to enter on the next line and for Macduff to obtain the prop head of Macbeth; *Retreat:* trumpet call for withdrawal or an end to fighting

64: **miss:** lack or need

65: **go off:** die; **by these I see:** by the number of forces I see still living

71: **unshrinking station:** refusal to yield or give ground

MACDUFF
    Then yield thee, coward,
    And live to be the show and gaze o' th' time.
    We'll have thee, as our rarer monsters are,
    Painted on a pole, and underwrit,   55
    "Here may you see the tyrant."

MACBETH
                 I will not yield,
    To kiss the ground before young Malcolm's feet,
    And to be baited with the rabble's curse.
    Though Birnam Wood be come to Dunsinane,
    And thou opposed, being of no woman born,   60
    Yet I will try the last. Before my body
    I throw my warlike shield. Lay on, Macduff,
    And damned be him that first cries "Hold, enough!"

                    Exeunt fighting. Alarums.
  Enter [MACBETH and MACDUFF] fighting, and Macbeth [is] slain.
           [MACDUFF exits carrying MACBETH's body.]
                            Retreat.
    Flourish. Enter, with drum and colors, MALCOLM,
        SIWARD, ROSS, THANES, and soldiers.

MALCOLM
    I would the friends we miss were safe arrived.

SIWARD
    Some must go off; and yet by these I see   65
    So great a day as this is cheaply bought.

MALCOLM
    Macduff is missing, and your noble son.

ROSS
    Your son, my lord, has paid a soldier's debt.
    He only lived but till he was a man,
    The which no sooner had his prowess confirmed   70
    In the unshrinking station where he fought,
    But like a man he died.

75: **hurts before:** wounded on the front of his body, rather than stabbed in the back

78: **fairer:** better

79: **knell is knolled:** funeral bell is tolled

81: **parted well, and paid his score:** died a good death and settled his accounts
i.e., acquitted himself nobly

82: Stage Direction: ***with Macbeth's head:*** Many productions from Davenant onward
have Macbeth killed onstage, and so the directions have had to be modified. In many
others, Macduff comes on not with Macbeth's head but with his (Macbeth's) sword,
dagger, or crown. However, original practice seems to call for the head to be
displayed, and we must remember that traitor's heads during Shakespeare's time
were displayed on pikes on London Bridge and other prominent locations.

85: **compassed:** surrounded; **pearl:** the nobility of Scotland

SIWARD

            Then he is dead?

ROSS

    Ay, and brought off the field. Your cause of sorrow
    Must not be measured by his worth, for then
    It hath no end.

SIWARD

            Had he his hurts before?   75

ROSS

    Ay, on the front.

SIWARD

            Why then, God's soldier be he.
    Had I as many sons as I have hairs,
    I would not wish them to a fairer death:
    And so, his knell is knolled.

MALCOLM

            He's worth more sorrow,
    And that I'll spend for him.

SIWARD

            He's worth no more   80
    They say he parted well, and paid his score,
    And so, God be with him. Here comes newer comfort.
                   Enter MACDUFF, with Macbeth's head

MACDUFF

    Hail, king! For so thou art. Behold, where stands
    The usurper's cursèd head. The time is free.
    I see thee compassed with thy kingdom's pearl,   85
    That speak my salutation in their minds,
    Whose voices I desire aloud with mine.
    Hail, King of Scotland!

All

    Hail, King of Scotland!

                                Flourish

90: **expense:** amount

91: **reckon with:** take account of

92: **make us even:** pay the debts I owe, that is, reward those who have served well

98: **Producing forth the cruel ministers:** bringing to justice the agents of Macbeth

100–101: **self and violent . . . life:** died violently by her own hand

3-4-6

MACBETH
Accursed be the tongue that tell me so   WARNING FOR CUE 11
And be these juggling fiends no more believed!
        (MACBETH falls dead. The derisive cackle
        of the WITCHES is heard. MACBETH has
        fallen so his body is hidden behind the
        battlements at the top of the tower.
        MACDUFF kneels behind this during the
        laughter and rises to silence it, hold-
        ing in his hand, MACBETH'S bloody head.
        MACDUFF throws the head into the mass
        of waving leaves below.)
                    MACDUFF
Hail, king!
        (At this the ARMY drops the branches and   CUE 11 - WORD CUE
        Jungle collapses; revealing a stage-
        full of people. MALCOLM is on the throne,
        crowned. ALL bow before him -- ALL but
        HECATE and the THREE WITCHES who stand
        above the body of LADY MACBETH. THEY
        have caught MACBETH'S head and they hold
        it high, triumphantly.)
For so thou art! Behold,
Where stands
The usurper's cursed head;
        (The WITCHES gleefully raise the head
        above them.)
The time is free!   CUE 12 - WORD CUE
Hail King of Scotland!

            VOICES OF VOODOO WOMEN
All Hail Malcolm ---

        (THEY are interrupted by the thunderous
        chorus of the army.)
                    ARMY
Hail, King of Scotland.   CUE 13 - WORD CUE

            VOODOO WOMEN
Thrice to mine and thrice to thine;
And thrice again to make up nine.
                    HECATE
Peace!
        (Drums, ARMY, music, VOODOO VOICES, ALL
        are instantly silent.)
The charm's wound up!

            C U R T A I N

The 1936 production at the New Lafayette Theatre directed by Orson Welles ends with the death of Macbeth and the witches' celebration

Library of Congress, Music Division, Federal Theatre Project Collection

MALCOLM

> We shall not spend a large expense of time   90
> Before we reckon with your several loves,
> And make us even with you. My thanes and kinsmen,
> Henceforth be earls, the first that ever Scotland
> In such an honor named. What's more to do,
> Which would be planted newly with the time,   95
> As calling home our exiled friends abroad
> That fled the snares of watchful tyranny,
> Producing forth the cruel ministers
> Of this dead butcher and his fiend-like queen,
> Who, as 'tis thought, by self and violent hands   100
> Took off her life. This, and what needful else
> That calls upon us, by the grace of Grace,
> We will perform in measure, time and place.
> So, thanks to all at once and to each one,
> Whom we invite to see us crowned at Scone.   105

Flourish. Exeunt.

The Cast Speaks

THE 2004–05 CAST FROM THE SHAKESPEARE
THEATRE COMPANY

Marie Macaisa

In the texts of his plays, directors, actors, and other interpreters of Shakespeare's work find a wealth of information. For example, in *Macbeth*, we know quite a bit about what leads the titular character to murder the king, Duncan. We see in the opening scene the three witches planning to meet Macbeth, and we observe them intrigue him with their prophecies. We hear his thoughts (as asides at the end of 1.3) when the first prophecy proves true. We hear Lady Macbeth voice her concerns about whether her husband's nature will allow him to fulfill the second prophecy, urging and daring him to act. We are privy to Macbeth's thoughts as he contemplates killing Duncan (soliloquy in 1.7.1–28), and finally, we hear him decide to commit the deed (the dagger speech in 2.1.34–65). Yet, the responsibility for Duncan's death remains open to interpretation. Is Macbeth a victim of the witches or his too-ambitious wife? Or is his destiny, as he himself admits, driven by his own "vaulting ambition"?

While providing extra information, Shakespeare (like all playwrights and unlike novelists) also leaves gaps. We are thus coaxed to fill in the missing information ourselves, either through reasonable surmises (we can guess that Lady Macbeth has had a child) or through back stories we devise on our own (perhaps the Macbeths had a baby who didn't survive). This mix—simultaneously knowing too much and not enough—enables us to paint vivid, varied interpretations of the same play.

In staging a play, a director creates a vision for his or her production starting from the text, but moves beyond that by making decisions on what *isn't* in the text. The director, in collaboration with the actors, fleshes out the characters: they discuss what they might be like, create stories that explain their actions, determine motivations, and speculate on the nature of their relationships. In Shakespeare they have a rich text upon which to draw and hundreds of years of performances for inspiration. Thus we, the audience, can experience a play anew each time we see it in a different production. Perhaps it is in an unfamiliar setting; perhaps it is in a scene or characterization we hadn't noticed in the past; perhaps it is in the realization that we have changed our opinions about the actions of the characters in the play. Whatever the case, a closer look into one cast's interpretation creates an opportunity for us to make up our own minds about their stories, and in the process, gain new insights not just into a centuries-old play, but quite possibly into ourselves as well.

SHAKESPEARE THEATRE COMPANY, WASHINGTON, D.C., 2004–05

In *Macbeth*, director Michael Kahn sees a focus on the personal, the internal repercussions of actions. Macbeth chooses a course of action that makes him uneasy and doubtful, while Lady Macbeth is so sure of herself that she is shocked out of her senses when she comes to the realization that she is wrong. Explains Kahn, "Macbeth starts out with a clear conscience, realizes the possible consequences of an action, goes ahead with it anyway, and it destroys him." By contrast, "his wife starts out not caring about consequences, but she discovers a conscience, and it destroys her." In this production, the pull of opposites and contradictions abound.

These interviews were conducted in May 2006, more than a year after the original run. The actors were interviewed individually and asked about their characters, their relationships, and a scene or two in which their character is key. Keep in mind that their answers represent but one interpretation of the play. You may be surprised; you may agree or disagree strongly with a point of view—but that is exactly the point.

Unlike traditional productions, the witches in this staging are not limited to a few scenes in the heath or around a cauldron. Rather, Kahn made the choice to integrate the witches tightly into the Macbeth household as servants. Largely unnoticed, they were able to observe the chain of events that began with their prophecies.

Witch: Naomi Jacobson

We were maids working in the household, so we were present throughout. We were cleaning and scrubbing the floors, serving at the banquet, working as gentlewomen. The three of us were part of the underprivileged class, turning to evil for power.

Witch: Jewell Robinson

We were humans, regular people who practiced witchcraft. We cast spells and worshiped the devil. Our portrayal also had sexual overtones; there was a lot of writhing.

As servants, we were always watchful, exchanging a lot of meaningful looks. We were also able to use our chores in the household as part of our witchcraft.

Witch: Sarah Marshall

We got a hold of a knife from the banquet scene, I remember, and used it for the cauldron ritual in the second act.

Witch: Naomi Jacobson:

And I was scrubbing the floor before the scene where Lady Macbeth awaits Macbeth after the murder of Duncan [2.2]. I leave the bucket filled with water there, and it becomes what he uses to wash his hands clean.

I play my witch as someone who is not quite sure about her powers, so everything is new and exciting to her. I am thrilled and mesmerized by the effects of my incantations. When Duncan arrives at the castle, I experience a kind of glee and anticipation that order will be upset and chaos will reign. What will happen and how will it go down? I want to get as close to it as possible. I was the waiting-gentlewoman in Lady Macbeth's sleepwalking scene with the doctor, and when she goes back to bed at the end, clearly disturbed, I struggle between wanting to follow her and keeping an acceptable public face for the doctor.

Witch: Jewell Robinson

We all feel a strong connection to Macbeth as well, and we provide the support for what he wants to do. We are present throughout his entire journey.

At the center of the production, according to Kahn, "is a man who is an extraordinary soldier—a brutal, extraordinary soldier who kills easily and violently for the service of his country. That kind of killing is not only accepted

Emery Battis as the Doctor, Naomi Jacobson as a gentlewoman, and Kelly McGillis as Lady Macbeth in the Shakespeare Theatre Company's 2004–05 production directed by Michael Kahn
Photo: Richard Termine

but also lauded because it preserves the society. Macbeth is also hugely ambi-tious, as we find modern generals often are. I think he and his wife want and expect him to be king, as the kingdom in Scotland was not passed down from father to son." Yet there was something in him that was broken.

Macbeth: Patrick Page

I imagine Macbeth to be a man who really needs his wife's love and approval. He loves her with every fiber of his being and is terrified of losing her. He's lived with that terror for quite a while. In rehearsal, we also dis-cussed what their situation was with respect to children. We know she has had a child [1.7.54–55: "I have given suck, and know / How tender 'tis to love the babe that milks me"], so we are left with a couple of possibilities. One is that they had a child together who died in infancy or later, and the other is that Lady Macbeth has had a child with a previous husband and they both died. We assume they've been married a while, so we decided he had the problem and that he is unable to father children.

Now, this is a man who is a great warrior, beloved by his men, and has enjoyed military success. Yet we decided he has a crippling level of insecurity and that's where it comes from. Despite his skills on the battlefield, he feels like he is less of a man.

According to Kahn, "If you are the kind of man that Macbeth is and you keep trying to have a child and you don't, your sense of your own manhood is threatened. If you're the kind of warrior that Macbeth is then I think you overcompensate, and I think that's the button that's being pushed in the very beginning because everyone knows that Lady Macbeth had a child and that child died."

Lady Macbeth: Kelly McGillis

Lady Macbeth was very much in love with her husband. Yes, she was ambitious, but she was also terribly fearful. Her only job description then was to have children and be a mother. She might have had a child before but not now and not with Macbeth. So in the past, she used to have an identity and a place in the world and now she has none. I think this is one of the reasons she is interested in becoming queen.

Patrick Page as Macbeth and Kelly McGillis as Lady Macbeth in the Shakespeare Theatre Company's 2004–05 production directed by Michael Kahn
Photo: Richard Termine

Macbeth: Patrick Page

I think Macbeth would have made a good king. He's the best strategist and he's an excellent fighter. However, his personal battle to be king is not about ambition but about manhood.

One of his greatest strengths is his imagination. He can picture an event in his mind in great detail and understand how it has to happen. It's real to him, and he can't make a distinction between what's occurring in his mind and the world. His body shuts down through the course of the play—he can't eat or sleep—further loosening his hold on reality.

Given that his imagination was central to this character, we felt that Banquo's Ghost should not appear in the banquet scene and that there should be no dagger. He sees them; we don't. If you put the ghost in the scene, then you are seeing what Macbeth sees versus what the other people see and what the play is concerned about. We want to show when and why others decide to act against Macbeth.

After Duncan's death, the lords don't know whom to trust and they are all initially suspicious of each other. They focus on Macbeth at different points, though sadly for Banquo, his uncertainty (perhaps he couldn't imagine his friend guilty of regicide) cost him his life.

Duncan: Ted van Griethuysen

Duncan was dressed entirely in white and gold and he represented "goodness" in the production. He stood for order and continuity of the true line. Whatever Macbeth was after, he was in the way.

I think he was a sensible king, though not a fighter who got his hands dirty. He trusted Macbeth and Lady Macbeth. As far as he knows, there was no reason to distrust them. Macbeth was a loyal warrior, trusted by others.

Porter: Ted van Griethuysen

The porter is at the opposite end of the scale from the king. He is an old drunk whose lone scene [2.3] is meant to be funny. The scene was staged almost as a shadow play. When I enter, I put the lantern downstage and I end up casting shadows on the wall. The images are at times funny, amusing, and even vulgar and lewd. At one point, the figure on the wall becomes a devil

Ted van Griethuysen as the porter in the Shakespeare Theatre Company's 2004–05 production directed by Michael Kahn
Photo: Richard Termine

and I end up scaring myself. It introduced the devil in a very clear, visual way. The porter could be the devil-porter to the gates of hell.

Thomas De Quincey wrote an excellent essay, "On the Knocking at the Gate," that was first published in 1823; our production is consistent with that. The knocking at the gate represents the intrusion of reality into the Macbeths' world of darkness and evil. When two people are alone in their dreams and intentions they can get far away from the real world and that lets them carry out what they must do. This knocking serves as a transition from their private world of murder and mayhem into the real, more orderly world of Macduff and the Thanes.

Banquo: Glenn Fleshler

Banquo is an honorable man, a foil to Macbeth in many ways; for example, Banquo is a loving father. In the beginning of Act 2, when he has had bad dreams and cannot sleep, he enters with his son, Fleance. He [Fleance] ends up falling asleep in that scene, and Banquo takes care of him. And of course, he fights to save his son even as he lay dying, shouting for him to "Fly, good Fleance, fly, fly, fly!" [3.3.17].

The rest of 2.1 is a conversation between Macbeth and Banquo; they are feeling each other out. On the one hand, they've fought side by side so you know they have some degree of mutual trust. On the other hand, Banquo has started to observe some strange behavior. He points this out when he says, "Look, how our partner's rapt" [1.3.142] when Macbeth is soliloquizing after he finds out he is now Thane of Cawdor.

I (me, the actor) try not to act like I know too much after Duncan's murder. Banquo is suspicious, but he's not sure. Every one of the Scottish lords is suspicious of each other, I think. There are a lot of glances going around when we're on stage.

After the coronation (between acts 2 and 3), Banquo's suspicions deepen and he has a speech that begins, "Thou hast it now—king, Cawdor, Glamis,

Kelly McGillis as Lady Macbeth and Patrick Page as Macbeth with the Ensemble in the Shakespeare Theatre Company's 2004–05 production directed by Michael Kahn
Photo: Richard Termine

all / As the weird women promised, and I fear, / Thou played'st most foully for't" [3.1.1–3]. Though I'm still not certain, and I try not to think of Macbeth as guilty when he enters, I'm clearly not anxious to go to the banquet.

Lennox: Glenn Pannell

Lennox is a younger and less experienced soldier than Macbeth, Banquo, or Macduff. I don't think he's participated in many battles. He's in awe of Macbeth—he's heard the tales of his bravery in battle and they've made an impression on him. He's loyal to the king, but he has his own opinions on how Scotland is being governed. After all, there is a reason they are under attack. He probably thinks Duncan is an ineffectual leader while Macbeth would be a great leader.

Nevertheless, Duncan's murder affects him. At first, he accepts without question the fiction that the grooms did it. He was the one to accompany Macbeth to confirm Macduff's discovery of Duncan and he presumably observed the slaying of the grooms. Macbeth's behavior at the banquet, however, gives him pause and that was when he started becoming suspicious. Afterwards, he has a scene [3.6] where he discusses the state of the kingdom with another lord (in our production, it was Angus), and he notes sarcastically how the deaths seem to have worked out very well for Macbeth. Still, none of the lords are quite sure who is with Macbeth or against so they all speak in code, in words that can be interpreted both ways.

Lennox is still in Macbeth's court the next time we see him; he gives Macbeth an update on Macduff's movements ["'Tis two or three, my lord, that bring you word / Macduff is fled to England" 4.1.142–143], so he clearly didn't act right away. After that, however, he appears with the other lords as part of the rebellion.

Angus: David Heuvelman

When we first see Angus, he is with Ross, bringing Duncan the news of the former Thane of Cawdor's traitorous actions. When Duncan bestows the title on Macbeth, he thinks it's a great thing. Macbeth deserves it, he's the best warrior, and they are behind him.

However, when Macbeth becomes king, Angus and the other lords are dissatisfied and there is unrest among them. They think it's possible he murdered Duncan, making him the worst tyrant imaginable. They don't believe that Malcolm and Donalbain were responsible for their father's death. After the banquet scene and Macbeth's disturbing behavior, he grows even more suspicious.

When Lennox and Angus are talking [in 3.6; Angus is the unnamed lord], I played it such that Angus at first believes that the official version of the events was true. But after Lennox's speech, by the time I inform him of Macduff going to find Malcolm and raising an army, I no longer believe it and I think Macduff's actions are a good thing. [3.6.32–37: "That, by the help of these…we may again / Give to our tables meat, sleep to our nights… receive free honors, / All which we pine for now."] It shows that he (and probably the other lords) is willing to rebel against the king and dethrone him.

Patrick Page as Macbeth and Samuel Bednar Schachter as Fleance in the Shakespeare Theatre Company's 2004–05 production directed by Michael Kahn
Photo: Richard Termine

Ross: Richard Pelzman

Ross is a great soldier, comparable to Banquo in skill and social standing. He's accomplished and respected, and is very impressed with Macbeth, who is the über soldier. He respects Duncan, is loyal to him, and has no anxiety or concerns that may cause him to think otherwise. As part of the traveling party (post-Macbeth's victory), he didn't have any intimation of the impending darkness.

After Duncan's death, Macbeth's killing of the grooms puzzles Ross. Why would he do such a thing? Ross's suspicions take root when he witnesses a seemingly innocuous moment between Macbeth and Fleance. Banquo and Fleance are saying goodbye before their ill-fated journey and Macbeth, goofing around with Fleance, playfully plops his crown on Fleance's head. At that moment, the entire mood changes and he grimly and quickly snatches it back. (This was not in the text or the stage direction, and Patrick Page did a masterful job of building a theatrical moment.)

Observing this and putting it together with his previous behavior [slaying the grooms], Ross begins to wonder about the murder of Duncan. Macbeth's behavior at the banquet confirms his suspicions, but it is not till after another event that he becomes active in the rebellion. That event is his delivering to Macduff the news of his family's savage slaughter.

We rehearsed that scene quite a bit and talked a lot about what my level of emotion should be, coming into the scene. In the end, we decided that simplest was best. Ross enters very solemnly, but not with an overwhelmingly ominous air. It is not until the specific line, "Your castle is surprised, your wife and babes / Savagely slaughtered" [4.3.205–206], that he gives in to the tragedy.

This scene is sort of a bookend to the opening scene, when I'm bestowing honor and sharing good news with Macbeth (that he is Thane of Cawdor). Here it is the opposite. I am imparting horrible news and supporting Macduff's decision to kill Macbeth.

Macduff: Andrew Long

The scene where I receive the news of my family's slaughter [starting from 4.3.159] was a very challenging one for me. It was extremely emotional and it fuels the rest of the play. You just have to go for it and be overwhelmed.

My lines are short and the ideas and underlying emotions shift rapidly: anger, grief, denial, vengeance, confusion. I had to take my time and experience each one instead of just emoting. As a peer, I thought Macbeth was worthy, but I was wrong. I go searching for Malcolm, who is the touchstone of what is good.

Brandon Demery as Malcolm, Andrew Long as Macduff, and Richard Pelzman as Ross in the Shakespeare Theatre Company's 2004–05 production directed by Michael Kahn
Photo: Richard Termine

The scene with him, before I get the news, is one of our director's favorites. Malcolm is testing me, and there's a lot of wordplay. He's not sure whether I can be trusted (for all he knows, I've been sent by Macbeth). Also, I was the one who discovered his father. Our director urged us to make our choices small and as specific as possible, so as not to give too much away.

I was very relieved at the end, when Malcolm admits his "false speaking" and tells me about the army of ten thousand readying to invade Scotland. Unfortunately, that relief lasts for just a very short moment.

Malcolm: Brandon Demery

When we first see Malcolm, he is introducing his father to the sergeant who saved him from captivity. So we know he was in the battle but was taken prisoner. He's not the warrior Macbeth is, but no one is.

When he is told that his father was murdered, his response is "O, by whom?" [2.3.94]. When I was saying those lines, I would look at Macbeth, almost making a passive-aggressive accusation. Donalbain and I feel very uneasy in that scene and we stay and talk after everyone leaves. I tell him I'm going to England [an unnamed lord later tells Lennox in 3.6.26–29 that Malcolm "Lives in the English court and is received / Of the most pious Edward with such grace" and that he is accorded high respect] and Donalbain tells me he's going to Ireland for the safety of us both. Neither of us knows whom we can trust and we both feel we're in danger because we are the murdered king's sons. His last lines to me are, "Where we are / There's daggers in men's smiles. The near in blood, / The nearer bloody" [2.3.133–135].

Glen Pannell as Lennox, Brandon Demery as Malcolm, Christopher Browne as Bloody Captain, Ted van Griethuysen as Duncan, Kip Pearson as Donalbain, and Randolph Adams as a soldier in the Shakespeare Theatre Company's 2004–05 production directed by Michael Kahn
Photo: Richard Termine

The next time I appear is in 4.3, when Macduff finds me. I don't know whether I can trust him so I put him through a test. As an actor, you really have to know your objective to navigate those tricky lines. It's a mystery what exact moment in that scene (or whether there is one) gives Malcolm the confidence that Macduff is okay, but he is finally convinced.

Malcolm would make a good king. He himself names the qualities of someone who would be a good leader and he demonstrates many of those qualities: "The king-becoming graces, / As justice, verity, temperance, stableness, / Bounty, perseverance, mercy, lowliness, / Devotion, patience, courage, fortitude" [4.3.91–94]. Malcolm is also pious, loyal to his family, and above all, loyal to his country. He finally confesses to Macduff, "What I am truly / Is thine and my poor country's to command."

While Malcolm and the troops are amassing and gaining strength, Macbeth and Lady Macbeth are headed in the opposite direction. Both are now unable to sleep, each of them is hallucinating and losing their grip on reality, and there is a strong sense that things are quickly and inevitably going out of control.

Lady Macbeth: Kelly McGillis
Everything she does is about control. And the more she acts to gain control (of her life, her destiny, her future) the more she realizes she doesn't have it. The sleepwalking scene [5.1] indicates a loss of control. Guilt is eating away at her and she has lost. Everything has gone awry.

Macbeth: Patrick Page
Harold Bloom suggests that the reason we're able to [sympathize] with Macbeth is because of his sense of outrage at being dealt a bad hand. I felt that outrage acutely at the end of the banquet scene. I had resolved that I was going to make things better; I would be a good king and ruler; my wife and I were now going to have a wonderful life. Banquo, whom I handled on my own, was going to be a good surprise for her, but here he is ruining everything. I keep trying to finish things off but they won't be finished.

Macbeth decides that the solution to this is to stop resisting. Instead he will embrace everything and go to the weird sisters. I have a long speech where I describe the unnatural things that have happened [4.1.50–61] and tell them it doesn't matter, to give me all the answers. In that scene, I take a blood oath and I am bound to them. By the time I have Macduff's family slaughtered, I am less than human.

Jewell Robinson as a witch and Patrick Page as Macbeth in the Shakespeare Theatre Company's 2004–05 production directed by Michael Kahn
Photo: Richard Termine

Director: Michael Kahn

Something happens when you begin to kill for personal reasons as opposed to political ones. *Macbeth* was written after the Gunpowder Plot [a failed attempt in 1605 by a group of English Catholics to blow up the Parliament, King James I, his family, and most of the Protestant aristocracy during the State Opening], so assassination was a big issue, and certainly this play was written to say assassination was a bad thing. But what's interesting is that the people who commit the assassination are not just given a straightforward villainous nature. They are given complexity. That seems to be a very radical idea—to talk about the killing of a king by a complicated person at a time when people were being hanged and drawn and quartered for attempting the same.

A Voice Coach's Perspective on Speaking Shakespeare

KEEPING SHAKESPEARE PRACTICAL

Andrew Wade

track 41–42

Introduction to Speaking Shakespeare: Derek Jacobi
Speaking Shakespeare: Andrew Wade with Drew Cortese

Why, you might be wondering, is it so important to keep Shakespeare practical? What do I mean by practical? Why is this the way to discover how to speak the text and understand it?

Plays themselves are not simply literary events—they demand interpreters in the deepest sense of the word, and the language of Shakespeare requires, therefore, not a vocal demonstration of writing techniques but an imaginative response to that writing. The key word here is imagination. The task of the voice coach is to offer relevant choices to the actor so that the actor's imagination is titillated, excited by the language, which he or she can then share with an audience, playing on that audience's imagination. Take the word "IF"—it is only composed of two letters when written, but if you say it aloud and listen to what it implies, then your reaction, the way the word plays through you, can change the perception of meaning. "Ifffffffff" . . . you might hear and feel it implying "possibilities," "choices," "questioning," "trying to work something out." The saying of this word provokes active investigation of thought. What an apt word to launch a play: "If music be the food of love, play on" (Act 1, Scene 1 in *Twelfth Night, or What You Will*). How this word engages the listener and immediately sets up an involvement is about more than audibility. How we verbalize sounds has a direct link to meaning and understanding. In the words of Touchstone in *As You Like It*, "Much virtue in if."

I was working with a company in Vancouver on *Macbeth,* and at the end of the first week's rehearsal—after having explored our voices and opening out different pieces of text to hear the possibilities of the rhythm, feeling how the meter affects the thinking and feeling, looking at structure and form— one of the actors admitted he was also a writer of soap operas and that I had completely changed his way of writing. Specifically, in saying a line like "The multitudinous seas incarnadine / Making the green one red," he heard the complexity of meaning revealed in the use of polysyllabic words becoming monosyllabic, layered upon the words' individual dictionary definitions. The writer was reminded that merely reproducing the speech of everyday life was nowhere near as powerful and effective as language that is shaped.

Do you think soap operas would benefit from rhyming couplets? Somehow this is difficult to imagine! But the writer's comments set me thinking. As I am constantly trying to find ways of exploring the acting process, of opening out actors' connections with language that isn't their own, I thought it would be a good idea to involve writers and actors in some practical work on language. After talking to Cicely Berry (Voice Director, Royal Shakespeare Company) and Colin Chambers (then RSC Production Adviser), we put together a group of writers and actors who were interested in taking part. It was a fascinating experience all round, and it broke down barriers and misconceptions.

The actors discovered, for instance, that a writer is not coming from a very different place as they are in their creative search; that an idea or an image may result from a struggle to define a gut feeling and not from some crafted, well-formed idea in the head. The physical connection of language to the body was reaffirmed. After working with a group on Yeats's poem "Easter 1916," Ann Devlin changed the title of the play she was writing for the Royal Shakespeare Company to *After Easter*. She had experienced the poem read aloud by a circle of participants, each voice becoming a realiza- tion of the shape of the writing. Thus it made a much fuller impact on her and caused her thinking to shift. Such practical exchanges, through language work and voice, feed and stimulate my work to go beyond making sure the actors' voices are technically sound.

It is, of course, no different when we work on a Shakespeare play. A similar connection with the language is crucial. Playing Shakespeare, in many ways, is crafted instinct. The task is thus to find the best way to tap into someone's imagination. As Peter Brook put it: "People forget that a text is dumb. To make it speak, one must create a communication machine. A living network, like a nervous system, must be made if a text which comes from far away is to touch the sensibility of the present."

This journey is never to be taken for granted. It is the process that every text must undergo every time it is staged. There is no definitive rehearsal that would solve problems or indicate ways of staging a given play. Again, this is where creative, practical work on voice can help forge new meaning by offering areas of exploration and challenge. The central idea behind my work comes back to posing the question, "How does meaning change by speaking out aloud?" It would be unwise to jump hastily to the end process for, as Peter Brook says, "Shakespeare's words are records of the words that he wanted spoken, words issuing from people's mouths, with pitch, pause and rhythm and gesture as part of their meaning. A word does not start as a word—it is the end product which begins as an impulse, stimulated by attitude and behavior which dictates the need for expression." [1]

PRACTICALLY SPEAKING

Something happens when we vocalize, when we isolate sounds, when we start to speak words aloud, when we put them to the test of our physicality, of our anatomy. We expose ourselves in a way that makes taking the language back more difficult. Our body begins a debate with itself, becomes alive with the vibrations of sound produced in the mouth or rooted deep in the muscles that aim at defining sound. In fact, the spoken words bring into play all the senses, before sense and another level of meaning are reached.

"How do I know what I think, until I see what I say," Oscar Wilde once said. A concrete illustration of this phrase was reported to me when I was leading a workshop recently. A grandmother said the work we had done that day reminded her of what her six-year-old grandson had said to his mother while they were driving through Wales: "Look, Mummy, sheep! Sheep! Sheep!" "You don't have to keep telling us," the mother replied, but the boy said, "How do I know they're there, if I don't tell you?!"

Therefore, when we speak of ideas, of sense, we slightly take for granted those physical processes which affect and change their meaning. We tend to separate something that is an organic whole. In doing so, we become blind to the fact that it is precisely this physical connection to the words that enables the actors to make the language theirs.

The struggle for meaning is not just impressionistic theater mystique; it is an indispensable aspect of the rehearsal process and carries on during the life of every production. In this struggle, practical work on Shakespeare is vital and may help spark creativity and shed some light on the way meaning is born into language. After a performance of *More Words*, a show devised and directed by Cicely Berry and myself, Katie Mitchell (a former artistic director of The Other Place in Stratford-upon-Avon) gave me an essay by Ted Hughes that echoes with the piece. In it, Ted Hughes compares the writing of a poem—the coming into existence of words—to the capture of a wild animal. You will notice that in the following passage Hughes talks of "spirit" or "living parts" but never of "thought" or "sense." With great care and precaution, he advises, "It is better to call [the poem] an assembly of living parts moved by a single spirit. The living parts are the words, the images, the rhythms. The spirit is the life which inhabits them when they all work together. It is impossible to say which comes first, parts or spirit."

This is also true of life in words, as many are connected directly to one or several of our senses. Here Hughes talks revealingly of "the five senses," of "word," "action," and "muscle," all things which a practical approach to language is more likely to allow one to perceive and do justice to.

Words that live are those which we hear, like "click" or "chuckle," or which we see, like "freckled" or "veined," or which we taste, like "vinegar" or "sugar," or touch, like "prickle" or "oily," or smell, like "tar" or "onion," words which belong to one of the five senses. Or words that act and seem to use their muscles, like "flick" or "balance." [2]

In this way, practically working on Shakespeare to arrive at understanding lends itself rather well, I think, to what Adrian Noble (former artistic director of the RSC) calls "a theater of poetry," a form of art that, rooted deeply in its classical origins, would seek to awaken the imagination of its audiences through love and respect for words while satisfying our eternal craving for myths and twice-told tales.

This can only be achieved at some cost. There is indeed a difficult battle to fight and hopefully win "the battle of the word to survive." This phrase was coined by Michael Redgrave at the beginning of the 1950s, a period when theater began to be deeply influenced by more physical forms, such as mime. [3] Although the context is obviously different, the fight today is of the same nature.

LISTENING TO SHAKESPEARE

Because of the influence of television, our way of speaking as well as listening has changed. It is crucial to be aware of this. We can get fairly close to the way *Henry V* or *Hamlet* was staged in Shakespeare's time; we can try also to reconstruct the way English was spoken. But somehow, all these fall short of the real and most important goal: the Elizabethan ear. How did one "hear" a Shakespeare play? This is hardest to know. My personal view is that we will probably never know for sure. We are, even when we hear a Shakespeare play or a recording from the past, bound irrevocably to modernity. The Elizabethan ear was no doubt different from our own, as people were not spoken to or entertained in the same way. A modern voice has to engage us in a different way in order to make us truly listen in a society that seems to rely solely on the belief that image is truth, that it is more important to show than to tell.

Sometimes, we say that a speech in Shakespeare, or even an entire production, is not well-spoken, not up to standard. What do we mean by that? Evidently, there are a certain number of "guidelines" that any actor now has to know when working on a classical text. Yet, even when these are known, actors still have to make choices when they speak. A sound is not a sound without somebody to lend an ear to it: rhetoric is nothing without an audience.

There are a certain number of factors that affect the receiver's ear. These can be cultural factors such as the transition between different acting styles or the level of training that our contemporary ear has had. There are also personal and emotional factors. Often we feel the performance was not well-spoken because, somehow, it did not live up to our expectations of how we think it should have been performed. Is it that many of us have a self-conscious model, perhaps our own first experience of Shakespeare, that meant something to us and became our reference point for the future (some treasured performance kept under glass)? Nothing from then on can quite compare with that experience.

Most of the time, however, it is more complex than nostalgia. Take, for example, the thorny area of accent. I remind myself constantly that audibility is not embedded in Received Pronunciation or Standard American. The familiarity that those in power have with speech and the articulate confidence gained from coming from the right quarters can lead us all to hear certain types of voices as outshining others. But, to my mind, the role of theater is at least to question these assumptions so that we do not perpetuate those givens but work towards a broader tolerance.

In Canada on a production of *Twelfth Night*, I was working with an actor who was from Newfoundland. His own natural rhythms in speaking seemed completely at home with Shakespeare's. Is this because his root voice has direct links back to the voice of Shakespeare's time? It does seem that compared to British dialects, which are predominantly about pitch, many North American dialects have a wonderful respect and vibrancy in their use of vowels. Shakespeare's language seems to me very vowel-aware. How useful it is for an actor to isolate the vowels in the spoken words to hear the music they produce, the rich patterns, their direct connection to feelings. North Americans more easily respond to this and allow it to feed their speaking. I can only assume it is closer to how the Elizabethans spoke.

In *Othello* the very names of the characters have a direct connection to one vowel in particular. All the male names, except the Duke, end in the sound OH: Othello, Cassio, Iago, Brabantio, etc. Furthermore, the sound OH ripples through the play both consciously and unconsciously. "Oh" occurs repeatedly and, more interestingly, is contained within other words: "so," "soul," and "know." These words resonate throughout the play, reinforcing another level of meaning. The repeating of the same sounds affects us beyond what we can quite say.

Vowels come from deep within us, from our very core. We speak vowels before we speak consonants. They seem to reveal the feelings that require the consonants to give the shape to what we perceive as making sense.

Working with actors who are bilingual (or ones for whom English is not the native language) is fascinating because of the way it allows the actor to have an awareness of the cadence in Shakespeare. There seems to be an objective perception to the musical patterns in the text, and the use of alliteration and assonance are often more easily heard not just as literary devices, but also as means by which meaning is formed and revealed to an audience.

Every speech pattern (e.g., accent, rhythm) is capable of audibility. Each has its own music, each can become an accent when juxtaposed against another. The point at which a speech pattern becomes audible is in the dynamic of the physical making of those sounds. The speaker must have the desire to get through to a listener and must be confident that every speech pattern has a right to be heard.

SPEAKING SHAKESPEARE

So, the way to speak Shakespeare is not intrinsically tied to a particular sound; rather, it is how a speaker energetically connects to that language. Central to this is how we relate to the form of Shakespeare. Shakespeare employs verse, prose, and rhetorical devices to communicate meaning. For example, in *Romeo and Juliet*, the use of contrasts helps us to quantify Juliet's feelings: "And learn me how to lose a winning match," "Whiter than new snow upon a raven's back." These extreme opposites, "lose" and "winning," "new snow" and "raven's back," are her means to express and make sense of her feelings.

On a more personal note, I am often reminded how much, as an individual, I owe to Shakespeare's spoken word. The rather quiet and inarticulate schoolboy I once was found in the speaking and the acting of those words a means to quench his thirst for expression.

NOTES:
(1) Peter Brook, *The Empty Space* (Harmondsworth: Penguin, 1972).
(2) Ted Hughes, *Winter Pollen* (London: Faber and Faber, 1995).
(3) Michael Redgrave, *The Actor's Ways and Means*
    (London: Heinemann, 1951).

In the Age of Shakespeare

Thomas Garvey

One of the earliest published pictures of Shakespeare's birthplace, from an original watercolor by Phoebe Dighton (1834)

The works of William Shakespeare have won the love of millions since he first set pen to paper some four hundred years ago, but at first blush, his plays can seem difficult to understand, even willfully obscure. There are so many strange words: not fancy, exactly, but often only half-familiar. And the very fabric of the language seems to spring from a world of forgotten assumptions, a vast network of beliefs and superstitions that have long been dispelled from the modern mind.

In fact, when "Gulielmus filius Johannes Shakespeare" (Latin for "William, son of John Shakespeare") was baptized in Stratford-on-Avon in 1564, English itself was only just settling into its current form; no dictionary had yet been written, and Shakespeare coined hundreds of words himself. Astronomy and medicine were entangled with astrology and the occult arts; democracy was waiting to be reborn; and even educated people believed in witches and fairies, and that the sun revolved around the Earth. Yet somehow Shakespeare still speaks to us today, in a voice as fresh and direct as the day his lines were first spoken, and to better understand both their artistic depth and enduring power, we must first understand something of his age.

REVOLUTION AND RELIGION

Shakespeare was born into a nation on the verge of global power, yet torn by religious strife. Henry VIII, the much-married father of Elizabeth I, had

From *The Book of Martyrs* (1563), this woodcut shows the Archbishop of Canterbury being burned at the stake in March 1556

Map of London ca. 1625

defied the pope by proclaiming a new national church, with himself as its head. After Henry's death, however, his daughter Mary reinstituted Catholicism via a murderous nationwide campaign, going so far as to burn the Archbishop of Canterbury at the stake. But after a mere five years, the childless Mary also died, and when her half-sister Elizabeth was crowned, she declared the Church of England again triumphant.

In the wake of so many religious reversals, it is impossible to know which form of faith lay closest to the English heart, and at first, Elizabeth was content with mere outward deference to the Anglican Church. Once the pope hinted her assassination would not be a mortal sin, however, the suppression of Catholicism grew more savage, and many Catholics— including some known in Stratford—were hunted down and executed, which meant being hanged, disemboweled, and carved into quarters. Many scholars suspect that Shakespeare himself was raised a Catholic (his father's testament of faith was found hidden in his childhood home). We can speculate about the impact this religious tumult may have had on his plays. Indeed, while explicit Catholic themes, such as the description of purgatory in *Hamlet*, are rare, the larger themes of disguise and double allegiance are prominent across the canon. Prince Hal offers false friendship to Falstaff in the histories, the heroines of the comedies are forced to disguise themselves as men, and the action of the tragedies is driven by double-dealing villains. "I am not what I am," Iago tells us (and himself) in *Othello*, summing up in a single stroke what may have been Shakespeare's formative social and spiritual experience.

If religious conflict rippled beneath the body politic like some ominous undertow, on its surface the tide of English power was clearly on the rise. The defeat of the Spanish Armada in 1588 had established Britain as a global power; by 1595 Sir Walter Raleigh had founded the colony of Virginia (named for the Virgin Queen), and discovered a new crop, tobacco, which would inspire a burgeoning international trade. After decades of strife and the threat of invasion, England enjoyed a welcome stability. As the national coffers grew, so did London; over the course of Elizabeth's reign, the city would nearly double in size to a population of some two hundred thousand.

Hornbook from Shakespeare's lifetime

A 1639 engraving of a scene from a royal state visit of Marie de Medici depicts London's packed, closely crowded half-timbered houses.

FROM COUNTRY TO COURT

The urban boom brought a new dimension to British life—the mentality of the metropolis. By contrast, in Stratford-upon-Avon, the rhythms of the rural world still held sway. Educated in the local grammar school, Shakespeare was taught to read and write by a schoolmaster called an "abecedarian," and as he grew older, he was introduced to logic, rhetoric, and Latin. Like most schoolboys of his time, he was familiar with Roman mythology and may have learned a little Greek, perhaps by translating passages of the New Testament. Thus while he never attended a university, Shakespeare could confidently refer in his plays to myths and legends that today we associate with the highly educated.

Beyond the classroom, however, he was immersed in the life of the countryside, and his writing all but revels in its flora and fauna, from the wounded deer of *As You Like It* to the herbs and flowers which Ophelia scatters in *Hamlet*. Pagan rituals abounded in the rural villages of Shakespeare's day, where residents danced around maypoles in spring, performed "mummers' plays" in winter, and recited rhymes year-round to ward off witches and fairies.

The custom most pertinent to Shakespeare's art was the medieval "mystery play," in which moral allegories were enacted in country homes and village squares by troupes of traveling actors. These strolling players—usually four men and two boys who played the women's roles—often lightened the moralizing with bawdy interludes in a mix of high and low feeling, which would become a defining feature of Shakespeare's art. Occasionally even a professional troupe, such as Lord Strange's Men, or the Queen's Men, would arrive in town, perhaps coming straight to Shakespeare's door (his father was the town's bailiff) for permission to perform.

Rarely, however, did such troupes stray far from their base in London, the nation's rapidly expanding capital and cultural center. The city itself had existed since the time of the Romans (who built the original London Bridge), but it was not until the Renaissance that its population spilled beyond its ancient walls and began to grow along (and across) the Thames, by whose banks the Tudors had built their glorious palaces. It was these two contradictory worlds—a modern metropolis cheek-by-jowl with a medieval court—that provided the two very different audiences who applauded Shakespeare's plays.

Londoners both high and low craved distraction. Elizabeth's court constantly celebrated her reign with dazzling pageants and performances that required a local pool of professional actors and musicians. Beyond the graceful landscape of the royal parks, however, the general populace was packed into little more than a square mile of cramped and crooked streets where theatrical entertainment was frowned upon as compromising public morals.

Just outside the jurisdiction of the city fathers, however, across the twenty arches of London Bridge on the south bank of the Thames, lay the wilder district of "Southwark." A grim reminder of royal power lay at the end of the bridge—the decapitated heads of traitors stared down from pikes at passersby. Once beyond their baleful gaze, people found the amusements they desired, and their growing numbers meant a market suddenly existed for daily entertainment. Bear-baiting and cockfighting flourished, along with taverns, brothels, and even the new institution of the theater.

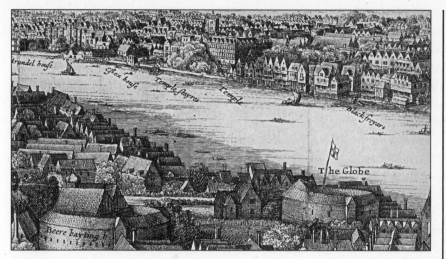

Southwark, as depicted in Hollar's long view of London (1647). Blackfriars is on the top right and the labels of bear-baiting and the Globe were inadvertently reversed.

THE ADVENT OF THE THEATRE

The first building in England designed for the performance of plays—called, straightforwardly enough, "The Theatre"—was built in London when Shakespeare was still a boy. It was owned by James Burbage, father of Richard Burbage, who would become Shakespeare's lead actor in the acting company, the Lord Chamberlain's Men. "The Theatre," consciously or unconsciously, resembled the yards in which traveling players had long plied their trade—it was an open-air polygon, with three tiers of galleries surrounding a canopied stage in a flat central yard, which was ideal for the athletic competitions the building also hosted. The innovative arena must have found an appreciative audience, for it was soon joined by the Curtain, and then the Rose, which was the first theater to rise in Southwark among the brothels, bars, and bear-baiting pits.

Even as these new venues were being built, a revolution in the drama itself was taking place. Just as Renaissance artists turned to classical models for inspiration, so English writers looked to Roman verse as a prototype for the new national drama. "Blank verse," or iambic pentameter (that is, a poetic line with five alternating stressed and unstressed syllables), was an adaptation of Latin forms, and first appeared in England in a translation of Virgil's *Aeneid*. Blank verse was first spoken on stage in 1561, in the now-forgotten *Gorboduc*, but it was not until the brilliant Christopher Marlowe (born the same year as Shakespeare) transformed it into the "mighty line" of such plays as *Tamburlaine* (1587) that the power and flexibility of the form made it the baseline of English drama.

Marlowe—who, unlike Shakespeare, had attended college—led the "university wits," a clique of hard-living free thinkers who in between all manner of exploits managed to define a new form of theater. The dates of Shakespeare's arrival in London are unknown—we have no record of him in Stratford after 1585—but by the early 1590s he had already absorbed the essence of Marlowe's invention, and begun producing astonishing innovations of his own.

While the "university wits" had worked with myth and fantasy, however, Shakespeare turned to a grand new theme, English history—penning the three-part saga of *Henry VI* in or around 1590. The trilogy was such a success that Shakespeare became the envy of his circle—one unhappy competitor, Robert Greene, even complained in 1592 of "an upstart crow...beautified with our feathers...[who is] in his own conceit the only Shake-scene in a country."

Such jibes perhaps only confirmed Shakespeare's estimation of himself, for he began to apply his mastery of blank verse in all directions, succeeding at tragedy (*Titus Andronicus*), farce (*The Comedy of Errors*), and romantic comedy (*The Two Gentlemen of Verona*). He drew his plots from everywhere: existing poems, romances, folk tales, even other plays. In fact a number of Shakespeare's dramas (*Hamlet* included) may be revisions of earlier texts owned by his troupe. Since copyright laws did not exist, acting companies usually kept their texts close to their chests, only allowing publication when a play was no longer popular, or, conversely, when a play was *so* popular (as with *Romeo and Juliet*) that unauthorized versions had already been printed.

Demand for new plays and performance venues steadily increased. Soon, new theaters (the Hope and the Swan) joined the Rose in Southwark, followed shortly by the legendary Globe, which opened in 1600. (After some trouble with their lease, Shakespeare's acting troupe, the Lord

pendeſt on ſo meane a ſtay. Baſe minded men all three
of you, if by my miſerie you be not warnd:for vnto none
of you (like mee) ſought thoſe burres to cleaue : thoſe
Puppets (I meane) that ſpake from our mouths, thoſe
Anticks garniſht in our colours. Is it not ſtrange, that
I, to whom they all haue beene beholding: is it not like
that you, to whome they all haue beene beholding, ſhall
(were yee in that caſe as I am now) bee both at once of
them forſaken ': Yes truſt them not : for there is an vp=
ſtart Crow, beautified with our feathers, that with his
Tygers hart wrapt in a Players hyde, ſuppoſes he is as
well able to bombaſt out a blanke verſe as the beſt of
you : and beeing an abſolute Iohannes fác totum, is in
his owne conceit the onely Shake-ſcene in a countrey.
O that I might intreat your rare wits to be imploied in
more profitable courſes : ſ let thoſe Apes imitate your
paſt excellence, and neuer more acquaint them with
your admired inuentions. I knowe the beſt huſband of

Greene's insult, lines 9–14

Chamberlain's Men, had disassembled "The Theatre" and transported its timbers across the Thames, using them as the structure for the Globe.) Shakespeare was a shareholder in this new venture, with its motto "All the world's a stage," and continued to write and perform for it as well. Full-length plays were now being presented every afternoon but Sunday, and the public appetite for new material seemed endless.

The only curb on the public's hunger for theater was its fear of the plague—for popular belief held the disease was easily spread in crowds. Even worse, the infection was completely beyond the powers of Elizabethan medicine, which held that health derived from four "humors" or internal fluids identified as bile, phlegm, blood, and choler. Such articles of faith, however, were utterly ineffective against a genuine health crisis, and in times of plague, the authorities' panicked response was to shut down any venue where large crowds might congregate. The theaters would be closed for lengthy periods in 1593, 1597, and 1603, during which times Shakespeare was forced to play at court, tour the provinces, or, as many scholars believe, write what would become his famous cycle of sonnets.

THE NEXT STAGE

Between these catastrophic closings, the theater thrived as the great medium of its day; it functioned as film, television, and radio combined as well as a venue for music and dance (all performances, even tragedies, ended with a dance). Moreover, the theater was the place to see and be seen; for a penny

Famous scale model of the Globe completed by Dr. John Cranford Adams in 1954. Collectively, 25,000 pieces were used in constructing the replica. Dr. Adams used walnut to imitate the timber of the Globe, plaster was placed with a spoon and medicine dropper, and 6,500 tiny "bricks" measured by pencil eraser strips were individually placed on the model.

you could stand through a performance in the yard, a penny more bought you a seat in the galleries, while yet another purchased you a cushion. The wealthy, the poor, the royal, and the common all gathered at the Globe, and Shakespeare designed his plays—with their action, humor, and highly refined poetry—not only to satisfy their divergent tastes but also to respond to their differing points of view. In the crucible of Elizabethan theater, the various classes could briefly see themselves as others saw them, and drama could genuinely show "the age and body of the time his form and pressure," to quote Hamlet himself.

In order to accommodate his expanding art, the simplicity of the Elizabethan stage had developed a startling flexibility. The canopied platform of the Globe had a trap in its floor for sudden disappearances, while an alcove at the rear, between the pillars supporting its roof, allowed for "discoveries" and interior space. Above, a balcony made possible the love scene in *Romeo and Juliet,* while still higher, the thatched roof could double as a tower or rampart. And though the stage was largely free of scenery, the costumes were sumptuous—a theater troupe's clothing was its greatest asset. Patrons were used to real drums banging in battle scenes and real cannons firing overhead (in fact, a misfire would one day set the Globe aflame).

With the death of Elizabeth, and the accession of James I to the throne in 1603, Shakespeare only saw his power and influence grow. James, who considered himself an intellectual and something of a scholar, took over the patronage of the Lord Chamberlain's Men, renaming them the King's Men; the troupe even marched in his celebratory entrance to London. At this pinnacle of both artistic power and prestige, Shakespeare composed *Othello*, *King Lear*, and *Macbeth* in quick succession, and soon the King's Men acquired a new, indoor theater in London, which allowed the integration of more music and spectacle into his work. At this wildly popular venue, Shakespeare developed a new form of drama that scholars have dubbed "the romance," which combined elements of comedy and tragedy in a magnificent vision that would culminate in the playwright's last masterpiece, *The Tempest*. Not long after this final innovation, Shakespeare retired to Stratford a wealthy and prominent gentleman.

Beyond the Elizabethan Universe

This is how Shakespeare fit into his age. But how did he transcend it? The answer lies in the plays themselves. For even as we see in the surface of his drama the belief system of England in the sixteenth century, Shakespeare himself is always questioning his own culture, holding its ideas up to the light and shaking them, sometimes hard. In the case of the Elizabethan faith in astrology, Shakespeare had his villain Edmund sneer, "We make guilty of our disasters the sun, the moon, and stars; as if we were villains on necessity." When pondering the medieval code of chivalry, Falstaff decides, "The better part of valor is discretion." The divine right of kings is questioned in *Richard II*, and the inferior status of women—a belief that survived even the crowning of Elizabeth—appears ridiculous before the brilliant examples of Portia (*The Merchant of Venice*) and Rosalind (*As You Like It*). Perhaps it is through this constant shifting of perspective, this relentless sense of exploration, that the playwright somehow outlived the limits of his own period, and became, in the words of his rival Ben Jonson, "not just for an age, but for all time."

track 43

Conclusion of the Sourcebooks Shakespeare
Macbeth: *Sir Derek Jacobi*

About the Online Teaching Resources

The Sourcebooks Shakespeare is committed to supporting students and educators in the study of Shakespeare. A website with additional articles and essays, extended audio, a forum for discussions, and other resources can be found (starting in August 2006) at www.sourcebooksshakespeare.com. To illustrate how the Sourcebooks Shakespeare may be used in your class, Jeremy Ehrlich, the head of education at the Folger Shakespeare Library, contributed an essay called "Working with Audio in the Classroom." The following is an excerpt:

One possible way of approaching basic audio work in the classroom is shown in the handout [on the site]. It is meant to give some guidance for the first-time user of audio in the classroom. I would urge you to adapt this to the particular circumstances and interests of your own students.

To use it, divide the students into four groups. Assign each group one of the four technical elements of audio—volume, pitch, pace, and pause—to follow as you play them an audio clip or clips. In the first section, have them record what they hear: the range they encounter in the clip and the places where their element changes. In the second section, have them suggest words for the tone of the passage based in part on their answers to the first. Sections three and four deal with tools of the actor. Modern acting theory finds the actor's objective is his single most important acting choice; an actor may then choose from a variety of tactics in order to achieve that objective. Thus, if a character's objective on stage is to get sympathy from his scene partner, he may start out by complaining, then shift to another tactic (asking for sympathy directly? throwing a tantrum?) if the first tactic fails. Asking your students to try to explain what they think a character is trying to get, and how she is trying to do it, is a way for them to follow this process through closely. Finally, the handout asks students to think about the meaning (theme) of the passage, concluding with a traditional and important tool of text analysis.

As you can see, this activity is more interesting and, probably, easier for students when it's used with multiple versions of the same piece of text. While defining an actor's motivation is difficult in a vacuum, doing so in relation to another performance may be easier: one Othello may be more concerned with gaining respect while another Othello may be more concerned with obtaining love, for instance. This activity may be done outside of a group setting, although for students doing this work for the first time I suggest group work so they will be able to share answers on some potentially thought-provoking questions . . .

For the complete essay, please visit www.sourcebooksshakespeare.com.

Acknowledgments

The series editors wish to give heartfelt thanks to the advisory editors of the series, David Bevington and Peter Holland, for their ongoing support, timely advice, and keen brilliance. Thank you as well to Michael Kahn, an advisor for *Macbeth*, for his insights into the play and for the cooperation of his team at the Shakespeare Theatre Company.

We are incredibly grateful to the community of Shakespeare scholars for their generosity in sharing their talents, collections, and even their address books. We would not have been able to put together such an august list of contributors without their help. First, sincere thanks to our text editor, William Proctor Williams, not just for his impeccable work, but also for sharing his passion with us. Thanks as well to Gregory Doran, Tom Garvey, Doug Lanier, and Andrew Wade for their marvelous essays. Extra appreciation goes to Doug Lanier for all his guidance and the use of his personal Shakespeare collection. We are grateful to William for his continuing guidance on textual issues, though any errors in this edition are ours.

We want to single out Tanya Gough, the proprietor of The Poor Yorick Shakespeare Catalog, for all her efforts on behalf of the series. She was an early supporter, providing encouragement from the very beginning and jumping in with whatever we needed. For her encyclopedic knowledge of Shakespeare on film and audio, for sharing her experience, for her continuing support, and for a myriad of other contributions too numerous to mention, we offer our deepest gratitude.

Our research was aided immensely by the wonderful staff at Shakespeare archives and libraries around the world: Susan Brock, Helen Hargest, and the staff at The Shakespeare Birthplace Trust; Jeremy Ehrlich, Bettina Smith, and everyone at the Folger Shakespeare Library; and Gene Rinkel, Bruce Swann, and Nuala Koetter from the Rare Books and Special Collections Library at the University of Illinois. These individuals were instrumental in helping us gather audio: Carly Wilford, Justyn Baker, and Janet Benson. The following are the talented photographers who shared their work with us: Donald Cooper, Gerry Goodstein, George Joseph, and Richard Termine. Thank you to Jessica Talmage at the Mary Evans Picture Library and to Tracey Tomaso at Corbis. We appreciate all your help.

From the world of drama, the following shared their passion with us and helped us develop the series into a true partnership between the artistic and academic communities. We are indebted to: Liza Holtmeier, Lauren Beyea, Catherine Weidner, Michael Kahn, and the team from the Shakespeare Theatre Company; Bridget Daley, Bonnie J. Monte, and the team from The Shakespeare Theatre of New Jersey; Helen Robson, Jane Tassell, Gregory Doran and staff at the Royal Shakespeare Company; the 2004–05 cast of *Macbeth* from the Shakespeare Theatre Company in Washington, D.C.; Nancy Becker of The Shakespeare Society; Drew Cortese, and Joe Plummer.

With respect to the audio, we extend our heartfelt thanks to our narrating team: our director, John Tydeman, our esteemed narrator, Sir Derek Jacobi, and the staff of Motivation Studios. John has been a wonderful, generous resource to us and we look forward to future collaborations. We owe a debt of gratitude to Nicolas Soames for introducing us and for being unfailingly helpful. Thanks also to the "Speaking Shakespeare" team: Andrew Wade, Drew Cortese, and Lyron Bennett for that wonderful recording.

Our personal thanks for their kindness and unstinting support go to our friends and our extended families.

Finally, thanks to everyone at Sourcebooks who contributed their talents in realizing The Sourcebooks Shakespeare–in particular: Samantha Raue, Todd Stocke, Michelle Schoob, Megan Dempster, Dan Williams, Fred Marshall, and Michael Ryder. Special mention to Melanie Thompson, assistant extraordinaire for the Sourcebooks Shakespeare, who jumped in mid-series, unfazed.

So, thanks to all at once and to each one (5.7.104)

Audio Credits

In all cases, we have attempted to provide archival audio in its original form. While we have tried to achieve the best possible quality on the archival audio, some audio quality is the result of source limitations. Archival audio research by Marie Macaisa. Narration script by Joe Plummer and Marie Macaisa. Audio editing by Motivation Sound Studios, Marie Macaisa, and Todd Stocke. Narration recording, audio engineering, and mastering by Motivation Sound Studios, London, UK. Recording for "Speaking Shakespeare" by Sotti Records, New York City, USA.

Narrated by Sir Derek Jacobi
Directed by John Tydeman
Produced by Marie Macaisa

The following are under license from Pavilion Records Ltd. All rights reserved.
Tracks 3, 6, 12, 15, 17, 18, 21, 23, 28, 31, 33, 36, 40

The following are under license from Naxos of America www.naxosusa.com
℗ HNH International Ltd. All rights reserved.
Tracks 4, 7, 9, 14, 20, 24, 29, 34, 37

The following are selection from The Complete Arkangel Shakespeare ℗ 2003, with permission of The Audio Partners Publishing Corporation. All rights reserved. Unabridged audio dramatizations of all 38 plays. For more information, visit www.audiopartners.com/shakespeare.
Tracks 11, 26, 39

"Speaking Shakespeare" courtesy of Andrew Wade and Drew Cortese.
Track 42

Photo Credits

Every effort has been made to correctly attribute all the materials reproduced in this book. If any errors have been made, we will be happy to correct them in future editions.

Images from the 1936 production at the New Lafayette Theatre directed by Orson Welles are courtesy of the Library of Congress, Music Division, Federal Theatre Project Collection. Photos are credited on the pages in which they appear.

Images from the 1937 production at the Old Vic directed by Michel Saint-Denis are courtesy of the Rare Book and Special Collections Library, University of Illinois at Urbana-Champaign. Photos are credited on the pages in which they appear.

Photos from the Shakespeare Theatre Company's 2004–05 production directed by Michael Kahn are copyright © 2006 Richard Termine. Photos are credited on the pages in which they appear.

Photos from The Shakespeare Theatre of New Jersey's 2004 production directed by Bonnie J. Monte are copyright © 2006 Gerry Goodstein. Photos are credited on the pages in which they appear.

Photos from *The Tragedy of Macbeth* (1971) directed by Roman Polanski and the 1960 production directed by George Schaefer are courtesy of Douglas Lanier. Photos are credited on the pages in which they appear.

Photos from the Public Theater's 1957 production directed by Stuart Vaughan and the Public Theater's 1974 production directed by Edward Berkeley are copyright © 2006 George E. Joseph. Photos are credited on the pages in which they appear.

Photos from the 1938 Royal Shakespeare Company production directed by B. Iden Payne, the 1949 Royal Shakespeare Company production directed by

About the Contributors

TEXT EDITOR

William Proctor Williams is professor of English emeritus at Northern Illinois University and senior lecturer in English at the University of Akron. He has received numerous grants and awards including a National Endowment for the Humanities research grant and a Senior Fulbright Research Fellowship; and in 2003–04, he was the Myra and Charlton Hinman Fellow at the Folger Shakespeare Library. He is currently at work on the New Variorum Edition of *Titus Andronicus*, a critical edition of the works of Cosmo Manuche, and a study of Dr. Zachariah Pasfield, who licensed books for the press from 1600 until 1610.

SERIES EDITORS

Marie Macaisa spent twenty years in her first career: high tech. She has a BS in computer science from the Massachusetts Institute of Technology and an MS in artificial intelligence from the University of Pennsylvania. She edited the first two books in the series, *Romeo and Juliet* and *Othello*, contributed the "Cast Speaks" essays for all previous volumes, and is currently at work on the upcoming books.

Dominique Raccah is the founder, president, and publisher of Sourcebooks. Born in Paris, France, she has a bachelor's degree in psychology and a master's in quantitative psychology from the University of Illinois. She also serves as series editor of *Poetry Speaks* and *Poetry Speaks to Children*.

ADVISORY BOARD

David Bevington is the Phyllis Fay Horton Distinguished Service Professor in the Humanities at the University of Chicago. A renowned text scholar, he has edited several Shakespeare editions including the *Bantam Shakespeare* in individual paperback volumes, *The Complete Works of Shakespeare* (Longman, 2003), and *Troilus and Cressida* (Arden, 1998). He teaches courses in Shakespeare, renaissance drama, and medieval drama.

Peter Holland is the McMeel Family Chair in Shakespeare Studies at the University of Notre Dame. One of the central figures in performance-oriented Shakespeare criticism, he has also edited many Shakespeare plays, including *A Midsummer Night's Dream* for the Oxford Shakespeare series. He is also general editor of Shakespeare Survey and co-general editor (with Stanley Wells) of Oxford Shakespeare Topics. Currently he is completing a book, *Shakespeare on Film*, and editing *Coriolanus* for the Arden 3rd series.

Michael Kahn has led the Shakespeare Theatre Company in Washington, D.C., for nineteen seasons as artistic director, creating what the *Wall Street Journal* calls "the nation's foremost Shakespeare company." In addition to leading the Shakespeare Theatre Company, he is also the Richard Rodgers Director of the Drama Division at Juilliard and the founder of the Academy for Classical Acting at The George Washington University.

ESSAYISTS

Gregory Doran is the Chief Associate Director of the Royal Shakespeare Company. He has been an associate director since 1996. In 2006, he directed a highly acclaimed production of *Antony and Cleopatra* as part of the Complete Works Festival in Stratford. His other productions include *Venus and Adonis* with Michael Pennington; *Othello* with Sello Maake Ka-Ncube and Antony Sher; and *All's Well That Ends Wells* with Dame Judi Dench. In 2002, he was artistic director of a series of rare Jacobean plays in the Swan Theatre, for which he received the Olivier Award for Outstanding Achievement of the Year. He is coauthor, with his partner, Sir Antony Sher, of *Woza Shakespeare!*, about their experience of mounting a production of *Titus Andronicus* at the Market Theatre in Johannesburg. In 2006, he will direct a version of *The Rape of Lucrece*, a new musical production of *The Merry Wives of Windsor* with Dame Judi Dench, and *Coriolanus* with Will Houston and Janet Suzman.

Thomas Garvey has been acting, directing, or writing about Shakespeare for over two decades. A graduate of the Massachusetts Institute of Technology, he studied acting and directing with the MIT Shakespeare Ensemble, where he played Hamlet, Jacques, Iago, and other roles, and directed *All's Well That Ends Well* and *Twelfth Night*. He has since directed and designed several other Shakespearean productions, as well as works by Chekhov, Ibsen, Sophocles, Beckett, Moliere, and Shaw. Mr. Garvey currently writes on theater for the *Boston Globe* and other publications.

Douglas Lanier is an associate professor of English at the University of New Hampshire. He has written many essays on Shakespeare in popular culture, including "Shakescorp Noir" in *Shakespeare Quarterly* 53.2 (Summer 2002) and "Shakespeare on the Record" in *The Blackwell Companion to Shakespeare in Performance* (edited by Barbara Hodgdon and William Worthen, Blackwell, 2005). His book *Shakespeare and Modern Popular Culture* (Oxford University Press) was published in 2002. He is currently working on a book-length study of cultural stratification in early modern British theater.

Andrew Wade was head of voice for the Royal Shakespeare Company from 1990 to 2003 and voice assistant director from 1987 to 1990. During this time he worked on 170 productions and with more than 80 directors. Along with Cicely Berry, Andrew recorded *Working Shakespeare* and the DVD series on *Voice and Shakespeare*, and he was the verse consultant for the movie *Shakespeare in Love*. In 2000, he won a Bronze Award from the New York International Radio Festival for the series *Lifespan*, which he codirected and devised. He works widely teaching, lecturing, and coaching throughout the world.